S0-BJK-180

TO SECURE THE BLESSINGS OF LIBERTY

American Academy of Religion

Studies in Religion

35

Editors
Charley Hardwick
James O. Duke

TO SECURE THE BLESSINGS OF LIBERTY

American Constitutional Law
and the New Religious Movements

WILLIAM C. SHEPHERD

THE CROSSROAD PUBLISHING COMPANY
&
SCHOLARS PRESS

The Crossroad Publishing Company
370 Lexington Avenue
New York, NY 10017

Scholars Press
101 Salem St., P.O. Box 2268
Chico, CA 95927

Library of Congress Cataloging in Publication Data

Shepherd, William C.
  To secure the blessings of liberty.

  (Studies in religion / American Academy of
Religion ; no. 35)
  Bibliography: p.
  Includes index.
  1. Religious liberty—United States. 2. United
States—Constitutional law. 3. Sects—Law and
legislation—United States. I. Title. II. Series: Studies in
religion (American Academy of Religion) ; no. 35.
KF4783.S55   342.73'0852   84-1347
                    347.302852
ISBN 0-8245-0664-2
ISBN 0-8245-0670-7 (pbk.)
ISBN 0-89130-733-8 (Scholars Press)
ISBN 0-89130-824-5 (Scholars Press : pbk.)

Printed in the United States of America

For Sam and Kate

CONTENTS

We the People of the United States, in Order to form a more perfect Union, establish Justice, insure domestic Tranquility, provide for the common defence, promote the general Welfare, and secure the Blessings of Liberty to ourselves and our Posterity, do ordain and establish this Constitution for the United States of America.

Foreword

William Chauncey Shepherd III was a man of many parts and passions, and he was in a hurry to make good on them. At age twenty five he had his Yale Ph.D., his first book out (*Man's Condition*), and his first job at Smith College doing what he loved best (well, next to golf), teaching good students. An inverse Cartesian, he had a day's work done by noon, a day's play on the green in the afternoon, and a day's conviviality (not excluding an indulged taste for the higher cordials, music, literature and pool) in the evening. He was the fastest study I have known. Who is to deny that he packed at least eighty years into his forty?

Like Thoreau, Bill Shepherd entered the world's woods deliberately to transact some private business, to drive life into a corner and make it answer as to whether it were mean or good; and if mean to hear its rattle in his throat and feel its coldness in his members, or if good to publish its comforts on his next walk. I do not know what answer he got or even that the enterprise has reached its term. But I know that he lived another Thoreauvian maxim: "Rescue the drowning and tie your shoe-strings." And one from Melville as well: ". . . we should rub each other's shoulder blades, and pass the universal thump around."

When Shepherd came to the University of Montana in 1972 at the age of thirty he had already rounded a major bend. He had laid aside the study of the theological forms that religious sensibility assumes in favor of two other forms. Effecting a scholarly career change, he entered upon the study of religion from the standpoint of the social sciences. In his first five Montana years he concentrated upon the forms of religious sensibility in the individual psyche, the psychology of religion. Controlling the literature quickly, he settled on such seminal thinkers as Freud, Norman O. Brown, Philip Rieff and James Hillman. In his last five years he turned to the resonations of those psychic forms in the *socius*, to the sociology of religion. Following upon the pioneering work of Sidney Mead and Robert Bellah, he was attracted to new modalities of "civil religion" in the wake of the 1960s. And that led him to his last and perhaps deepest passion, the new religious movements, or "cults."

Himself a nonconformist and a dissenter from orthodoxies, Bill Shepherd was endlessly fascinated with the psychic processes, and their social consequences, of those drawn to what Justice Jackson described (and

Shepherd certainly concurred) as "mental and spiritual poison." His fascination was part and parcel of a larger preoccupation with "adherence," "deviance" and "cohesion," as these function in the formation of styles of life and religious communities. However appalled he was, and he was, at the commitments the young were willing, even eager to make, in the new religious movements, he was even more appalled at the reactions within contemporary American society to such commitments. Especially alarming to him were ominous signs that the judiciary would place within the prosecutor's, or the conservator's, reach what the first and related amendments to the Constitution had placed beyond law and its force, the inalienable right of individual choice in matters of religious belief and, within limits precedentially established, practice.

This book arose from that passion, and he cared deeply for what was and is at stake.

As the constitutional and legal dimensions of this passion were developed initially in conversations with his wife, a practicing attorney, so it is fitting that she should bring the book which embodies that passion to completion. On his death, Shepherd's manuscript was virtually complete in respect of his argument and the marshalling of evidence therefor. But much work remained to be done, and those closest to the project were of one mind that the person best suited to bring the book to press, by reason of her knowledge of the law and her skill with limpid prose, was Molly Shepherd. Bill often said that the book could not have originated without her; he did not know that it could not have ended without her as well. As we celebrate his life and this work, we are in her debt.

Ray L. Hart

Introduction

This book had its beginnings in 1980 when William C. Shepherd, Professor of Religious Studies at the University of Montana, was asked to teach a course on the Constitution and the new religious movements. He had been an observer of the new religions at least since 1972, and had published a number of scholarly articles on counter-cultural religiosity and on the processes of conversion and adhesion. Most notably, his article "The New Religions and the Religion of the Republic" appeared in 1978 in the *Journal of the American Academy of Religion.*

Professor Shepherd was awarded a B.A. from Dartmouth College in history and a Ph.D. from Yale University in religious studies. He was not formally trained in the law, but was the son of a distinguished practicing attorney and had grown up with respect and understanding for what judges and lawyers do. He caught on quickly to the intricacies of legal research, and more remarkably, to what is at stake in constitutional adjudication. The course he was asked to teach at the University of Montana was well attended, and was soon dubbed "The Courts and the Cults." He found the subject matter compelling and resolved to write a book addressing judicial treatment of new religious movement issues.

After writing several chapters, Professor Shepherd applied for and was awarded a grant by the National Endowment for the Humanities in order to complete his book. He spent the 1981–82 academic year as a visiting scholar at the Center for the Study of New Religious Movements in Berkeley, California. An abbreviated version of the first three chapters of his book was published in 1982 in the *Journal of the American Academy of Religion* under the title "The Prosecutor's Reach: Legal Issues Stemming from the New Religious Movements." At the time of his death in August, 1982, he had completed ten of eleven projected chapters.

As his widow and as a lawyer, I have edited and revised the chapters Bill Shepherd had written and have added a concluding chapter. I have also interpolated cases and commentary that Bill had not considered or that had not been published at the time of his death. In addition, I have modified the title of the book, which he had tentatively named "The Prosecutor's Reach: American Constitutional Law and the New Religious Movements." He had borrowed the title from Justice Jackson's dissent in *United States v. Ballard*, which is quoted at the beginning of the book and woven into subsequent chapters. Although I recognize the metaphorical value of "The Prosecutor's Reach," I feel it is too suggestive of criminal law and may inadvertently mislead the reader. Bill's book is about vindication of private rights in civil proceedings, not criminal ones. I hope the title I have substituted—*To Secure the Blessings of Liberty: American Constitutional Law and the New Religious Movements*—conveys more accurately the content of his book.

My overriding concern in completing the book has been to preserve and, if possible, to enhance the subtlety and integrity of Bill Shepherd's argument. He was convinced that invasion of a person's right to believe in any religious doctrine violates not only first amendment guarantees but more fundamentally, a person's right to treatment as an equal. Thus, inquisitorial examination into the truth or falsity of the belief of an adherent of a despised religious group must be forbidden, since it deprives the adherent of his right to the equal concern and respect of the law. Bill realized that there may be circumstances in which governmental intrusion into actions stemming from religious belief may be warranted. The Jonestown homicides provide the most notorious example. But before the government may intervene to impede free exercise of religion, it must demonstrate grave abuses endangering paramount social policy interests.

On an expansive reading, *To Secure the Blessings of Liberty* explores our commitment to constitutional rights when they clash with asserted social policy concerns. New religious movement legal cases provide a particularly precise means of gauging the depth of our commitment, for these cases pit one of our most fundamental and venerated liberties against strongly held majoritarian values. Bill Shepherd argues that both as a moral and as a legal matter, individual liberties must take precedence over utilitarian perceptions of the public good. In the chapters that follow, he celebrates cases in which judges have rejected assertions of the general welfare in favor of adherence to constitutional principle. He also decries those cases—and there are many—in which judges have acceded to prevailing prejudice and permitted intrusion on first and fourteenth amendment guarantees.

This book does not pretend to be an encyclopedic treatment of the new religious movements and the law. For example, it does not address the recent rash of damage suits against the new religions. Instead the book focuses on preserving and securing the liberties of citizens who happen to be members of socially scorned religious groups.

The following brief review of the contents of the book is offered to assist the reader. Chapter One examines the religion clauses of the first amendment as they have been interpreted by the Supreme Court. Chapter Two applies the principles derived from Supreme Court decisions to new religious movement litigation. Chapter Three investigates possible grounds for governmental intervention into the affairs of the new religions; in particular, it addresses arguments in favor of intervention advanced by "cult" critic Richard Delgado. Chapter Four describes the social context of new religious movement litigation. Chapter Five sets forth a theory of individual rights, drawn principally from the work of jurisprudential scholar Ronald Dworkin. The following three chapters are concerned with the Ku Klux Klan Act of 1871, which provides a potential federal remedy to new religious group members whose individual rights have been abridged by private conspirators. Thus Chapter Six analyzes congressional intent in passing the Klan Act; Chapter Seven reports on initially restrictive judicial construction of the Act; and Chapter Eight elaborates upon the expanded reading of the Act made possible by the Supreme Court's 1971 decision in *Griffin v. Breckenridge*. Chapter Nine examines cases brought by forcibly deprogrammed members of the new religions seeking to vindicate their constitutional rights. Chapter Ten challenges the propriety of imposing conservatorships in order to sanction deprogramming. Finally, Chapter Eleven endeavors to place new religious movement litigation within the framework of current Supreme Court interpretations of the scope of individual liberties.

Bill Shepherd would have been disturbed by the recent Supreme Court decisions addressed in the final chapter. These decisions vault judicial perceptions of the public good over private rights, thereby threatening the primacy of the latter. The Court's decision in *United Brotherhood of Carpenters v. Scott* particularly calls into question the viability of the Klan Act remedy for vindication of private rights, for which Bill argued strenuously. The decisions do not undercut the validity and the tenability of his argument, however. If anything, they bear out the observation he makes throughout the book: individual liberties are fragile and endlessly difficult to secure in practice.

$$* \quad * \quad * \quad * \quad *$$

It is never a simple matter to acknowledge fully the hand that others have had in the making of a book. It is especially difficult to do so with this book, for Bill Shepherd is not here to express his gratitude to the many people who extended their personal, scholarly, financial and technical support to him. I shall attempt here to acknowledge the support of those I know were instrumental in the undertaking, and ask the forgiveness of those who may have been omitted unintentionally.

First, numerous friends and colleagues have contributed both personal and scholarly assistance. On Bill's behalf, particular acknowledgment must go to Professors Ray L. Hart and James Flanagan, Bill's colleagues in the Department of Religious Studies at the University of Montana; to Professor Jacob Needleman and the staff of the Center for the Study of New Religious Movements; to Professor Thomas Robbins, who was Bill's colleague at the Center and who has continued to advise me on developments in the field; to Professors Charley D. Hardwick of American University, Jon Driessen of the University of Montana, Richard Delgado of the University of California at Los Angeles, and James T. Richardson of the University of Nevada at Reno; to attorney Jeremiah Gutman of New York City; and to Dr. Lee Coleman of Berkeley, California. Bill would also surely acknowledge the personal support he received from Kathleen Dugan in the months preceding his death. I wish to express particular personal gratitude to Ray L. Hart, president of the American Academy of Religion, for his invaluable advice and forbearance in the aftermath of Bill's death and for writing the foreword to this book. I am similarly grateful to William H. Forbis, author and former senior editor of *Time Magazine*, who cast his experienced copy editor's eye on the following pages and made substantial contributions to their clarity and accessibility.

Second, I must thank the National Endowment for the Humanities, Crossroads Publishing Company, and the Society for the Scientific Study of Religion for their respective financial contributions toward the completion of Bill's book.

Third, recognition must go to the capable and dedicated secretaries who typed the various drafts of the book. Lynne Carlisle and Jean Harte of the Department of Religious Studies at the University of Montana typed Bill's initial drafts. Linda J. Mamber, word processor in the law firm of Worden, Thane & Haines, P.C., my employer, typed the final drafts and must be given special credit for her thoroughness, competence and endurance.

Finally, this book is dedicated to Bill's children, Samuel and Katrina Shepherd. One cannot help but be reminded of the Preamble to the Constitution of the United States, from which the title of this book derives: To "secure the Blessings of Liberty to ourselves and our Posterity."

Molly R. Shepherd

PART I

The Law
and the New Religious Movements

Chapter 1

The Free Exercise Clause of the First Amendment

In his renowned dissent in *United States v. Ballard*, Justice Jackson made the following observations concerning the reach of the first amendment guarantee of free exercise of religion:

> There appear to be persons—let us hope not many—who find refreshment and courage in the teachings of the "I Am" cult. If the members of the sect get comfort from the celestial guidance of their "Saint Germain," however doubtful it seems to me, it is hard to say that they do not get what they pay for. Scores of sects flourish in this country by teaching what to me are queer notions. It is plain that there is wide variety in American religious taste. The Ballards are not alone in catering to it with a pretty dubious product.
>
> The chief wrong which false prophets do to their following is not financial. The collections aggregate a tempting total, but individual payments are not ruinous. I doubt if the vigilance of the law is equal to making money stick by over-credulous people. But the real harm is on the mental and spiritual plane. There are those who hunger and thirst after higher values which they feel wanting in their humdrum lives. They live in mental confusion or moral anarchy and seek vaguely for truth and beauty and moral support. When they are deluded and then disillusioned, cynicism and confusion follow. The wrong of these things, as I see it, is not in the money the victims part with half so much as in the mental and spiritual poison they get. But that is precisely the thing the Constitution puts beyond the reach of the prosecutor, for the price of freedom of religion or of speech or of the press is that we must put up with, and even pay for, a good deal of rubbish. (322 U.S. 78, 94–95, 1944)

Guy Ballard and several "I Am" movement adherents had been convicted of fraud for using the mails to promote their putative faith-healing powers. On appeal, the Supreme Court held that the jury could inquire into the sincerity, but not the truth or falsity, of the defendants' religious beliefs. Writing for the majority, Justice Douglas reiterated the Court's traditional, relatively restrictive conception of governmental power when conflicts arise between a secular interest of the state and activities carried out under the banner of the first amendment's guarantee of free religious exercise. The first amendment provides in its entirety:

> Congress shall make no law respecting an establishment of religion, or prohibiting the free exercise thereof; or abridging the freedom of speech, or of the press; or the right of the people peaceably to assemble, and to petition the Government for a redress of grievances.

Although the first amendment speaks directly only to Congress, the Supreme Court has made the amendment's prohibitions applicable to the states through incorporation of their principles into the due process clause of the fourteenth amendment.

Protection of the elderly and gullible from pilferage by charlatans was the secular interest implicated in *United States v. Ballard*. Extending the majority's rationale, the United States government might have exercised its police power to prevent a Jonestown-like tragedy. Knowing full well about the Jonestown suicide drills, the government might have intervened to prevent the homicides of children. But barring something resembling this extreme case, the courts may not attempt to judge the truth or falsity of any person's religious beliefs. As Justice Douglas wrote in his majority opinion in *Ballard*:

> Heresy trials are foreign to our Constitution. Men may believe what they cannot prove. They may not be put to the proof of their religious doctrines or beliefs. Religious experiences which are as real as life to some may be incomprehensible to others. Yet the fact that they may be beyond the ken of mortals does not mean that they can be made suspect before the law. . . . If one could be sent to jail because a jury in a hostile environment found one's teachings false, little indeed would be left of religious freedom. . . . The religious views espoused by respondents might seem incredible, if not preposterous, to most people. But if those doctrines are subject to trial before a jury charged with finding their truth or falsity, then the same can be done with the religious beliefs of any sect. When the triers of fact undertake that task, they enter a forbidden domain. (322 U.S. at 86–87)

This understanding of the judiciary's role in adjudicating clashes between religions and the state takes account of the constitutional wall protecting religious freedom. But until the 1960s, important decisions that attempted to balance first amendment religious rights against legitimate concerns of the state were weighted in favor of the latter.

A series of nineteenth-century cases challenging Mormon practices illustrates the Supreme Court's reluctance to confront issues stemming from the free exercise clause. In *Reynolds v. United States* (98 U.S. 145, 1878), the Court considered a free exercise challenge to a statute making bigamy punishable as a crime. Reynolds, a Mormon, contended he should be exempt from criminal punishment because polygamy was a tenet of his religion. The Court refused to countenance his plea on the ground that religious beliefs could not justify his exemption from a weighty secular commitment—the inviolable sanctity of the monogamous family. According to the Court, "[l]aws are made for the government of actions, and while they cannot interfere with mere religious belief and opinions, they may with practices" (*id.* at 166). Thus, the Mormons could believe whatever they chose, but as the Court later remarked in *Davis v. Beason* (133 U.S. 333, 341–42, 1890), to advocate polygamy "is to offend the common sense of mankind."

The Mormon cases were easy. Prevailing popular opinion was pitted against this persecuted minority group, and the offense was clear and statutorily forbidden. Sheer membership in the group became outlawry, and all Mormon land was forfeited to the government pursuant to the Court's decision in *Late Corporation of the Church of Jesus Christ of Latter-Day Saints v. United States* (136 U.S. 1, 65–66, 1890).

Even though the Court largely ducked the free exercise clause in its opinions in the Mormon cases, it coined a distinction between religious belief and religiously motivated practices that has been reiterated and reaffirmed in subsequent interpretations of the reach of the first amendment. For example, in *Cantwell v. Connecticut*, a 1940 Jehovah's Witnesses public solicitation case, the Court remarked:

> Thus the [First] Amendment embraces two concepts—freedom to believe and freedom to act. The first is absolute but, in the nature of things, the second cannot be. Conduct remains subject to regulation for the protection of society. (310 U.S. 296, 303–4, 1940)

Cases featuring Jehovah's Witnesses, Southern Protestant snake handlers, and Orthodox Jews further exemplify the Court's unwillingness prior to the 1960s to encounter directly the substantive challenge laid down by the free exercise clause. In *Minersville School District v. Gobitis* (310 U.S. 586, 1940), the Supreme Court upheld the expulsion of school children who refused to salute the American flag. Jehovah's Witnesses could count on freedom to believe what they wished provided patriotism was not compromised by their children's failure to pay proper obeisance to the flag. What was at stake in this rather typical case was a request for exemption from a statutory requirement for religious reasons. A conflict between the secular interest in patriotism and religious freedom of action based on belief was clearly joined. Three years later, in *West Virginia State Board of Education v. Barnette* (319 U.S. 624, 1943), the Court flatly overruled *Gobitis* and forbade compulsion in flag saluting ceremonies. But the reversal hinged on freedom of expression rather than on the free exercise clause. Justice Jackson expressly denied that the issue turned on "one's possession of particular religious views or the sincerity with which they are held" (*id.* at 634).

The context of the *Gobitis* and *Barnette* decisions helps explain the reversal. In 1940, Jehovah's Witnesses were the object of public censure.

By 1943, however, the Japanese and Germans appeared far more threatening than a few disobedient school children. Such rapid swings in popular opinion are also apparent in the chronicles of the "cult problem." For example, public fury against cults appeared to have waned in the late 1970s only to be rekindled by Jonestown in the fall of 1978.

Many southern Protestant groups, particularly in Appalachia, have long taken the Biblical text literally:

> And these signs shall follow them that believe: In my name shall they cast out devils; they shall speak with new tongues.
>
> They shall take up serpents; and if they drink any deadly thing, it shall not hurt them; they shall lay hands on the sick, and they shall recover. (Mark 16:17–18)

Handling poisonous rattlesnakes and drinking strychnine have as a consequence been fairly common practices among rural white people in pockets of the South (see LaBarre, *passim*). Here, the issues that have come before the courts do not involve requests for exemption from a state requirement due to a religiously based proscription, but rather requests for permission to carry out a religiously conceived obligation that is prohibited by the state (Burkholder: 35). The simple issue in *Bunn v. North Carolina* (336 U.S. 942, 1949) was whether protecting public safety outweighed upholding religious free exercise. Without discussion, the state court had concluded that of course the safety of the public must come first, and had sustained an ordinance prohibiting snake-handling. The Supreme Court, also without comment, dismissed the appeal for want of a substantial federal question.

One more example of earlier priority afforded secular concerns by the courts is in order. Some of the so-called "Sunday Law Cases" have dealt with Orthodox Jews who refuse to work on Saturday, their Sabbath. *Braunfeld v. Brown* (366 U.S. 599, 1961) is a leading and typical case of this sort. The Supreme Court upheld Pennsylvania Sunday closing laws, even though they imposed an economic burden on Orthodox Jewish merchants whose religious beliefs required that they close their shops on their own Sabbath day as well. The Court insisted that the resulting financial sacrifice was more an inconvenience than a substantial inroad on religion. The burden on religion was only indirect, because Judaism does not positively oblige working on Sunday. Furthermore, according to the Court, the Pennsylvania law had secular goals rather than religious ones, and therefore did not establish the Christian religion by preferential treatment (Pfeffer, 1967:281–87). Justice Brennan's dissent in *Braunfeld* did anticipate one plank in subsequent decisions, namely, that there must be a compelling state interest to override freedom of religious exercise (366 U.S. at 613–14). He challenged the majority's deference to the claimed secular interest in Sunday closings:

In fine, the Court, in my view, has exalted administrative convenience to a constitutional level high enough to justify making one religion economically disadvantageous. The Court would justify this result on the ground that the effect on religion, though substantial, is indirect. The Court forgets, I think, a warning uttered during the congressional discussion of the First Amendment itself: '... the rights of conscience are, in their nature, of particular delicacy, and will little bear the gentlest touch of governmental hand. ...' (*Id.* at 615–16)

Only in the last twenty years, as the issues confronting the Supreme Court have become more complex and delicate, has the Court evolved a body of doctrine that seeks neither to intrude wrongfully on religious exercise nor to ignore vital secular interests. Earlier conflicts between government and religions were relatively straightforward compared with those that arise time and again in the new religious movement cases. Prior to the 1960s, the Court most often was able to handle religious freedom claims simply by distinguishing between belief and the actions that follow from belief. Even more significant, governmental secular interests were never joined directly against free exercise claims standing alone. So fairly stark and untroublesome decisions were possible, either because state interests seemed quite compelling to the Court, or because other constitutional provisions buttressed free religious exercise and offered alternative grounds for decision.

But with the case of *Sherbert v. Verner* (374 U.S. 398, 1963), the Supreme Court broke new and significant constitutional ground. The free exercise clause was successful in its own right, and the theory developed in this crucial case has offered the decisive means for adjudicating new religious movement issues.

The Court held in *Sherbert* that denial of unemployment benefits to a Sabbatarian whose religious beliefs prevented her from accepting employment requiring work on Saturday was an impermissible burden on the free exercise of her religious beliefs. The state had failed to assert the nature of its interest at the trial level; on appeal, the state claimed that such an exemption would encourage fraudulent claims of religious infringement to avoid work and collect benefits. The Supreme Court stated that such an interest, if supported by evidence, would prevail provided the state could then prove that its interest could be protected by no less restrictive means. Because South Carolina had failed to support its stance, however, the Court refused to find that the state's interest was frustrated by allowing benefits to be paid.

Justice Brennan, writing for the Court, grounded the decision on a careful interpretation of the free exercise guarantee. First, Adell Sherbert's sincerity was stipulated. Second, Justice Brennan acknowledged that prohibition of Saturday labor is a "basic tenet" of the Seventh-Day

Adventists (374 U.S. at 399 n. 1). Further, since Mrs. Sherbert's religiously based conduct was made more difficult by the choice either to work on Saturday or to forego unemployment benefits, she was being forced by the state toward abandoning the practice of her religion. The final and most telling question raised by Brennan was whether some compelling state interest justified the considerable infringement of her first amendment rights.

> It is basic that no showing merely of a rational relationship to some colorable state interest would suffice; in this highly sensitive constitutional area, "[o]nly the gravest abuses, endangering paramount interests, give occasion for permissible limitation,". . . . No such abuse or danger has been advanced in the present case. . . . [I]t would plainly be incumbent upon the appellees to demonstrate that no alternative forms of regulation would combat . . . abuses without infringing First Amendment rights. (*Id.* at 406–7)

Sherbert's reasoning "requires the state to afford substantial deference to religiously motivated behavior" (Note, 53 *N.Y.U. L. Rev.* at 1261). The decision of the Court in *Wisconsin v. Yoder* (406 U.S. 205, 1972) confirmed the mandate. In *Yoder*, the Court acknowledged the state's "paramount" interest in educating its citizens—education is necessary, as the state argued, to prepare persons to participate in our political system and to enable those individuals to be self-reliant and self-sufficient. But Chief Justice Burger, writing for the Court, held that a state law requiring compulsory high school education was an impermissible burden on the Amish religion, because forced assimilation of Amish children into public high schools would undermine the Amish community and religious practices.

> They have carried the . . . difficult burden of demonstrating the adequacy of their alternative mode of continuing informal vocational education in terms of precisely those overall interests that the State advances in support of its program of compulsory high school education. (*Id.* at 235)

Further, the Court insisted that exemption from compulsory high school education for Amish children would not impair their physical or mental health or "in any other way materially detract from the welfare of society" (*id.* at 234). Finally, the state had failed to show "how its admittedly strong interest in compulsory education would be adversely affected by granting an exemption to the Amish" (*id.* at 236).

In *Yoder*, the Court explicitly applied the balancing test it had developed in *Sherbert*. The Court strove neither to "deny the free exercise of religious belief," nor to ignore "a state interest of sufficient magnitude to override the interest claiming protection under the Free Exercise Clause" (*id.* at 214). And again the religious liberty provision of the

Constitution stood successfully, establishing a belated, but now secure, precedent that all courts faced with religious issues must heed.

> Read in conjunction with *Sherbert*, *Yoder* can be seen to have substantially expanded the scope and operation of the free exercise clause, rousing it finally from its long dormancy. By upholding the religious liberty claim *Yoder* established that *Sherbert* was no aberration, and that progeny would follow. (Note, 53 *N.Y.U. L. Rev.* at 1263)

The Supreme Court's recent decision in *Thomas v. Review Board* (450 U.S. 707, 1981) again confirmed that *Sherbert* was no aberration. Thomas was a Jehovah's Witness who quit his job on the ground that his religious beliefs prevented him from participating in the production of armaments. The state denied his application for unemployment compensation benefits, asserting that a termination motivated by religion did not satisfy the "good cause" requirement imposed by the state unemployment compensation statute. The Court reversed the denial, finding the coercive impact on Thomas' free exercise rights "undistinguishable" from that found in *Sherbert* (*id*. at 717). And as in *Sherbert*, the interests advanced by the state did not justify the burden placed on free exercise:

> '[O]nly those interests of the highest order . . . can overbalance legitimate claims to the free exercise of religion.' (*Id*. at 718–19, quoting from *Wisconsin v. Yoder*, 406 U.S. at 215)

What has become known as the *Sherbert-Yoder* test was utilized effectively in defense of first amendment rights in a potpourri of cases during the 1970s. Allowances were made for the requests of many religious persons, including conscientious objectors wanting exemptions from ROTC, Indians wanting to wear braids in prison, and Jews wanting to sport beards in military service (for these and other cases, see Note, 53 *N.Y.U. L. Rev.* at 1264 nn. 118–20). Elements of the *Sherbert-Yoder* mechanism for balancing interests may be put into play either all together or singly as circumstances demand. In brief, the following questions are posed:

(1) Are the religious beliefs in question sincerely held?

(2) Are the religious practices under review germane to the religious belief system?

(3) Would carrying out the state's wishes constitute a substantial infringement on the religious practice?

(4) Is the interest of the state compelling? Does the religious practice perpetuate some grave abuse of a statutory provision or obligation?

(5) Are there alternative means of regulation by which the state's interest is served but the free exercise of religion is less burdened?

The states can regulate activities integral to the practice of one's sincerely held religious beliefs only if the regulation is the least restrictive means of promoting some compelling state interest. This is the judicial context in which the rights of members of currently unpopular new religious movements must be considered. When their religious activities are in conflict with some state interest, they are protected to these extents by the free exercise clause of the first amendment as clarified by *Sherbert-Yoder*.

Even before *Sherbert*, however, conflicts between the free exercise and establishment clauses of the first amendment proved troublesome. To the extent that state authorities accommodate religious interests of some part of the population, they may abridge the establishment clause which forbids preferential treatment of one religion over another. Cases involving military chaplains, aid to parochial schools, and exclusion of the teaching of evolution exemplify the considerable overlap, if not direct conflict, between the two religion clauses. Only recently, as in *Sherbert*, *Yoder* and *Thomas*, has the free exercise clause been treated with the same gravity as the establishment clause.

It is true that new conflicts have arisen as a result of the emergence of the free exercise clause. But in the wake of the *Sherbert* and *Yoder* decisions, the cardinal principle behind American constitutional law dealing with religion has been solidified: voluntarism. A religion may advance its interests with no support from the state, so the establishment clause stands firm. And by the same token, a religion advances only on the basis of the voluntary free choices of its members, so the free exercise clause has gained its rightful preeminence. Jefferson's "wall of separation" has now been erected by the case law as well, but it is more a thin line than a solid wall. Strictly speaking, separatism should mean complete nonentanglement or completely mutual abstinence between the churches and the state, but simple neutrality is unworkable. It is necessary to carve out a "zone of required accommodation" (Tribe: 821). Free exercise is the key. Governmental actions may be compelled in order to protect free exercise, but other state actions may be forbidden by both the free exercise and establishment clauses.

Several cases illustrate the principle. In *Illinois ex rel. McCollum v. Board of Education* (333 U.S. 203, 1948), the Court held that released time for religious instruction in a secular school classroom was impermissible because the state would thereby lend its weight in support of religion. On the other hand, such released time was held allowable if the instruction were carried out elsewhere (*Zorach v. Clauson*, 343 U.S. 306, 1952). Again a zone of accommodation was defined in *Everson v. Board of Education* (330 U.S. 1, 1947), in which the Court held that busing of children to parochial schools at public expense was permissible. But in *Epperson v. Arkansas* (393 U.S. 97, 1968), the Court ruled that a state statute prohibiting the teaching of evolution was unconstitutional because it preferred fundamentalist sectarian doctrine.

The chief impetus for the recent emergence of the free exercise clause is its importance for protecting despised and unpopular religious minorities from majoritarian persecution. The Supreme Court has adopted a broad functional definition of religion for free exercise purposes. As constitutional scholar Laurence Tribe contends:

> This functional approach has become a significant protection for unpopular and unconventional sects and represents an important development if the free exercise clause is to continue to fulfill its 'historic purpose.' (830)

It is vital for the new religious movement cases that the free exercise principle predominate in any conflict with anti-establishmentarianism. Religion should be tolerated as broadly as possible rather than thwarting at all costs any appearance of establishment. The purpose of disentanglement and anti-establishment is to make active provision for maximum diversity. In present circumstances, as opposed to those at the time of framing the Constitution, Professor Tribe argues that "religious tolerance must cease to be simply a negative principle and must become a positive commitment that encourages the flourishing of conscience" (834).

Lemon v. Kurtzman (403 U.S. 602, 1971) is a leading case circumscribing governmental action toward religion: the action of the state must be justifiable in secular terms. Governmental action, for example, in the distribution of textbooks must have a secular purpose, its effect must be primarily secular, and it must avoid excessive entanglement with religious authorities. Put the opposite way, any non-secular effect must be "*remote, indirect and incidental*" (Tribe: 840, emphasis in original).

Evolution of doctrine from the *Reynolds* polygamy case has come a long way. It is now apparent that no simple belief/action dichotomy will suffice in a complex society that requires governmental decisions about religion, but that permits only those decisions whose effects are primarily secular and do not prefer the religious interests of some over others. Protecting religious autonomy has now become the leading constitutional precept. One of the important ramifications of *Sherbert* was that the Court protected religious free exercise even when the state had imposed merely a negative burden; ineligibility for unemployment benefits because of a religious obligation not to work on Saturday was weighted as heavily as a positive governmental demand infringing religious belief. As Laurence Tribe puts it:

> [F]ailure to accommodate religion when the government could substantially achieve its legitimate goals while granting religious exemptions has been disapproved as hostility toward religion rather than hailed as the essence of neutrality. (852, passage italicized in original)

Together with *Yoder*, *Sherbert* has significantly expanded the meaning of the free exercise clause of the first amendment, and the government's interest in abridging it must now be extraordinarily weighty.

Another spin-off of *Sherbert, Yoder, Cantwell, Ballard* and other cases of less importance is that the state now has authority to press religious believers about their sincerity in only the most minimal way. The web of connections between a believer's faith and the sincerity with which he holds it is too close to admit of much adjudicatory discrimination. Justice Jackson recognized this phenomenon in his dissent in *Ballard*:

> [A]s a matter of either practice or philosophy I do not see how we can separate an issue as to what is believed from considerations as to what is believable. (322 U.S. at 92)

And as Tribe observes:

> [A]ny such inquiry can be extraordinarily dangerous. The perception of the claimant's sincerity inevitably reflects the factfinder's view of the reasonableness of the claimant's beliefs. Especially given the widening understanding of what constitutes religion in our society, the very rights ostensibly protected by the free exercise clause might well be jeopardized by any but the most minimal inquiry into sincerity. (861)

The core meaning of the religious clauses of the first amendment is that the government may neither pursue a religious goal nor impede the legal religious undertakings of its citizens. States may supply separable secular services such as busing, but not services that require constant surveillance to see if religion is somehow being bootlegged in (Tribe: 870). As the *Ballard* Court among others has made obvious:

> [T]he most clearly forbidden entanglement between church and state is the entanglement that occurs when institutions of civil government attempt to discover religious error by legal process, or to promulgate religious truth by legal decree.... [C]ivil authorities must abstain from religious controversies, so that each side of such a controversy can 'flourish according to the zeal of its adherents and the appeal of its dogma,' not according to its access to the levers of civil power. (Tribe: 871, quoting *Zorach v. Clauson*, 343 U.S. at 313)

Heresy is legal under United States law. The state may no more measure religious truth than it may inquire into the truth or falsity of a believer's faith, however bizarre such religious holdings may appear to the majority of citizens. Courtrooms may not become the arenas for the pursuit of persecutory zeal nor the forums for religious bigotry.

Chapter 2
The Free Exercise Clause
and the New Religious Movement Cases

The most typical and important of the new religious movement cases have involved parental petitions for temporary conservatorship or guardianship orders over adult children who have joined new religious groups. Although statutes vary from state to state, conservatorship laws commonly provide a means by which one person can obtain legal control over the person or property of another, and sometimes both. Statutory grounds for imposition of a conservatorship have to do with various sorts of incapacitation, including advanced age, mental impairment, illness, injury or other circumstances rendering one unable to care for one's self or property. Sometimes statutory grounds are so broad as to invite exploitation: prior to its amendment in 1977, California's conservatorship statute provided that an individual "likely to be deceived or imposed upon by artful or designing persons" was as much a candidate for conservatee status as the most hardened and helpless drug addict or severely disabled stroke victim (formerly Cal. Prob. Code § 1751, Deering 1959).

Katz v. Superior Court (73 Cal. App. 3d 952, 141 Cal. Rptr. 234, 1977) is the chief new religious movement conservatorship decision. The case involved five adult members of Reverend Sun Myung Moon's Unification Church, whose parents asked a California superior court for temporary conservatorship orders granting them authority over their children for a thirty-day period. The parents intended to use the time to subject their respective offspring to deprogramming procedures to be provided by the Freedom Ranch Rehabilitation Center of the Freedom of Thought Foundation in Tucson, Arizona. Each parental petition alleged that appointment was required because of the proposed ward's "mental illness or weakness and unsound mind" and propensity "to be deceived by artful and designing persons" (73 Cal. App. 3d at 962, 141 Cal. Rptr. at 239).

Following a hearing, the superior court granted the parents' petitions for temporary conservatorship orders. Counsel for the parents had argued that the five Moonists were victims of "psychological kidnapping" and "coercive conversion" accomplished through "fear and guilt tactics" (73 Cal. App. 3d at 972–73, 141 Cal. Rptr. at 246). Witnesses included a set of parents, two former Unification Church members, a psychiatrist (Dr. Samuel Benson), and a psychologist (Margaret Singer). Benson testified that symptoms displayed by the five included "memory impairment," blunted affect, "short attention spans and a decreased ability to concentrate," vagueness and "limited ability towards abstractions," paranoia about previous relationships, "defensive attitudes toward id urges," loss of "inner sense of authority," and "various degrees of regression and childlike attitudes." These problems, he continued, resulted from "coercive persuasion," "brainwashing" techniques borrowed from accounts of Korean and Vietnamese war prisoners (73 Cal. App. 3d at 976–77, 141 Cal. Rptr. at 248–49). Singer used pictures that she had had the Moonists draw as the basis for her remarks. She testified that they were victims of artful and designing persons; that their subjection to coercive persuasion amounted to an emergency situation; and that all were in need of treatment by the Freedom Ranch branch of "reality therapy" (73 Cal. App. 3d at 978, 141 Cal. Rptr. at 249).

Each of the proposed conservatees testified in opposition to the conservatorship petitions, and their employed psychiatrist and psychologist attempted to counter the testimony of the pair hired by their parents. Their psychiatrist questioned the propriety and application of the "artful and designing person test" (73 Cal. App. 3d at 979–80, 141 Cal. Rptr. at 250). Their psychologist testified that an emergency situation did not exist (*id.*).

The superior court judge did not reckon with the *Sherbert-Yoder* test in granting the temporary conservatorship orders: in fact, he did not address constitutional questions at all. The judge simply held for the parents because of the special sanctity of parent-child ties. In announcing his decision, he declared:

> '[W]e're talking about the very essence of life here, mother, father and children. There's nothing closer in our civilization. This is the essence of civilization.' (Quoted at 73 Cal. App. 3d at 963 n. 8, 141 Cal. Rptr. at 240 n. 8)

Several of the temporary conservatees petitioned for relief from the superior court order, and a California court of appeals granted their request. The appellate court first found that the "likely to be deceived by artful and designing persons" language of the California statute in effect at the time of the superior court hearing was unconstitutionally vague.

> In the field of beliefs, and particularly religious tenets, it is difficult, if not impossible, to establish a universal truth against which deceit and imposition can be measured. (73 Cal. App. 3d at 970, 141 Cal. Rptr. at 244)

The court next found that California's statute, even prior to its July,

1977 amendment, had not authorized the conservatorship appointments. According to the court, there was no emergency—"no real showing here that the conservatees are physically unhealthy, or actually deprived of, or unable to secure food, clothing and shelter" (73 Cal. App. 3d at 981, 141 Cal. Rptr. at 251). Equal protection and due process of the law forbid involuntary confinement in such instances (see further, Levine, 1974; and Coleman and Solomon, 1976).

> If there is coercive persuasion or brainwashing which requires treatment, the existence of such a mental disability and the necessity of legal control over the mentally disabled person for the purpose of treatment should be ascertained after compliance with the protection of civil liberties provided by the Welfare and Institutions Code. To do less is to license kidnapping for the purpose of thought control. (73 Cal App. 3d at 983, 141 Cal. Rptr. at 253)

Finally, the appeals court held that the temporary conservatorship orders violated the conservatees' rights to freedom of religion and association. The court examined precedent to establish that the conduct sought to be regulated stemmed from religious conviction; that investigation into whether conviction was induced by faith or by coercive persuasion was tantamount to forbidden investigation into the validity of faith; that an assumption of faithful motivation for proselytizing activities of church leaders must stand in the absence of evidence to the contrary; and that even if the organization were deemed political rather than religious, its members were guaranteed freedom of association by the first amendment (73 Cal. App. 3d at 984–88, 141 Cal. Rptr. at 253–56).

Referring to *Sherbert v. Verner* and *Wisconsin v. Yoder* (see Chapter 1), the court declared that the state could not interfere with the liberty of the Moonists unless it could advance a compelling state interest such as preventing fraud or protecting health. None was forthcoming. So "in the absence of such actions as render the adult believer himself gravely disabled," state processes "cannot be used to deprive the believer of his freedom of action and to subject him to involuntary treatment" (73 Cal. App. 3d at 988–89, 141 Cal. Rptr. at 256).

The *Katz* appeals court's application of the *Sherbert-Yoder* test is by no means perfect, particularly because it fails to distinguish between allowable inquiry into the sincerity with which a religious belief is held, and impermissible questions regarding the nature or content of the belief itself. *Katz* nevertheless adequately recognizes the burden that the state must meet in order to justify conservatorship orders constraining new religious movement group members. The appellate decision therefore is a baseline for the analysis of arguments in favor of state intervention to "rescue" nontraditional group adherents.

Neither the superior court nor the appellate court in *Katz* questioned the religious character of the Unification Church, and therefore its right to protection under the first amendment. Probably no court today could deprive any of the new nontraditional groups of religious status. The conscientious objector cases of *United States v. Seeger* (380 U.S. 163, 1965) and *Welsh v. United States* (398 U.S. 333, 1970) established the so-called "parallel position" rule, placing into constitutional practice a broad functional definition of religion along with a twin "ultimate concern" rule. So long as a sincere and meaningful belief occupies in the possessor's life a place parallel to that filled by commonly accepted ideas of God, and so long as beliefs are not based on "policy, pragmatism, or expediency," then they are constitutionally religious. "Religious beliefs may draw on a philosophical source, but the distinguishing characteristic of religion is the intensity of conviction with which the beliefs are held" (Shapiro: 759). All new "cultic" movements qualify, including quite nontheistic Eastern ones.

Sherbert-Yoder's sincerity aspect apparently has been more difficult for courts to apply. Sometimes it is not treated as a distinct part of the test. The *Katz* appellate judge, for example, overlapped inquiry into sincerity and inquiry into conduct, and needlessly marred the distinction between sincerity of group leaders and that of group members. Even if adherents are grossly deceived and are sustained in their faith by egregious threats and promises, their sincerity for legal purposes might still be above suspicion; vice versa, cult leaders might be flagrantly dedicated solely to exploitation and remunerative gain, yet their motives have no bearing on the sincerity of converts to their movements. Furthermore, questioning of cult members in conservatorship proceedings may not overstep clearly defined constitutional bounds. Cautious inquiry is allowed in an effort to ascertain a believer's sincerity (*United States v. Kahane*, 396 F.Supp. 687, E.D.N.Y. 1975). But no believer is required to demonstrate his competence or his mental health if these are challenged simply by virtue of his profession of religious faith. This most serious error of the *Katz* trial court was expressly corrected on appeal.

> The court explained why the conservatorships were unconstitutional by emphasizing that the superior court had overstepped its bounds when it imposed its judgment of the merits of the converts' religious convictions.
>
> Because the courts may not inquire into the wisdom of the theological tenets, a conservatorship order, which requires a determination of mental competence, may not be based on an inquiry into the substance of an adult's religious belief. Sanity or incompetence cannot, under the Constitution, be established by proof that one's religious faith is absurd. (Note, 53 N.Y.U. L. Rev. at 1269)

While its constitutional sensitivity was far from faultless, the *Katz* appellate court did get straight the most significant portion of a legitimate sincerity inquiry.

So far as degrees of state interference are concerned, scarcely any doubt can exist that conservatorship orders over adults pose enormous impositions on the course of day-to-day life. This is so even in cases that do not involve forcible deprogramming techniques such as food and sleep deprivation, constant barrages of anticult lectures, and physical threats. (See Patrick, 1976, *passim*, and 1979; and the documents in Pritchard, 1978. Various autobiographical accounts of deprogramming episodes are also available—see, *e.g.*, Underwood, 1979, and Edwards, 1979). Since conservators generally have extensive powers over the person, his whereabouts, his contacts, and even his reading matter, the inroads on freedom are obviously substantial.

> A conservatorship is not merely an indirect or incidental inconvenience—such as not receiving unemployment benefits or suffering a loss of revenue would be—but a total and direct denial of the members' ability to practice their religion and a serious threat to the freedom of their co-religionists. (Note, 53 N.Y.U. L. Rev. at 1272; also see Dean Kelley's remarks, Pritchard, 1977:3–23)

According to the Supreme Court's decisions in *Sherbert* and *Yoder*, the state's interest can prevail on this front only if the attendant infringement on religious liberty is not great; it is undeniably great where conservatorships are granted, and the state's burden is correspondingly heavy (Note, 53 *N.Y.U. L. Rev.* at 1272). The appellate court in *Katz* recognized but did not elaborate upon this point.

What grounds has the state to intervene in a person's life at the request of, say, his or her parents? The theoretical answer lies in the way the American tradition has developed the legal doctrine of *parens patriae. Parens patriae* simply means that the king, in his role as father of his country, has power to act on behalf of disabled people under his sovereignty. By extension, in American law the state may assume jurisdiction to care for those unable to care for themselves. This sounds innocuous enough, but for Nicholas Kittrie (among many other critics) the American embrace of *parens patriae* in recent decisions has opened the way to a "therapeutic revolution" involving a continuing relinquishment of the sanctions and powers of the criminal justice system to the therapists and hospitals (Kittrie: 3–4 and *passim*, and Coleman and Solomon). Helping those who cannot help themselves of course springs from benevolent motivation on the part of the states. The concern expressed by civil libertarians, however, is that *parens patriae* powers bypass due process constraints that must be met when the state acts pursuant to its police power in criminal proceedings. Thus enforced therapy rather than determinate sentencing becomes a powerful tool of control, not an instrument of rehabilitation (Coleman and Solomon: 346).

The risks of abuse are geometrically greater when *parens patriae* state authority is vested in a conservator for the purpose of therapeutic intervention into the religious beliefs of a person. Involuntary civil commitment of those the state deems dangerous or mentally ill requires no conviction of guilt; but at least the state is exercising its interest in protecting the general welfare in a direct way (see Levine, 1974). Where state power shifts to conservators, the possibilities for unjust and illegal deprivation of freedom are multiplied.

> Remitting a person to the care of a private guardian may leave him more vulnerable to impermissible influences than placing him in the care of the state. (Shapiro: 773)

Moreover, when individuals are brought to the attention of the judiciary solely because of their religious preferences, then first amendment protections clearly ought to come into play. Any state action is constitutionally questionable.

On occasion, the state has exercised *parens patriae* power to require, for example, medical treatment or vaccinations despite religious objections. The circumstances usually have involved potential threats to public peace or order, or dangers to parties other than the individual (for cases, see Note, 53 N.Y.U. L. Rev. at 1275 n. 170 and 1277 n. 181). The far knottier question is an ancient one, and the *Katz* case faced it directly: "does the state have an interest in protecting its *adult* citizens against *voluntary* harm to themselves?" (*id.* at 1276, emphasis in original). Can individuals jeopardize themselves if their conduct harms no one else? Does *parens patriae* power allow the state to interfere with fundamental rights because of its overriding interest in protecting its citizens even when their activities endanger only themselves? Answering negatively, *Sherbert* adopted a more or less libertarian position by permitting state action only in situations of "gravest abuses endangering paramount interests" (374 U.S. at 406).

Some content has been poured into the *Sherbert* rule by more recent cases. For example, a California appellate court refused to require a woman seeking disability benefits to undergo an operation prohibited by her religious beliefs. The court recognized the state's interest in the health of its citizens, but declared:

> [I]t is generally held that the courts . . . do not have the power to protect that interest by compelling treatment of a sane, conscious adult against the adult's wishes. . . . When considerations of conscience grounded upon religious beliefs are involved, the state interest in preserving health pales into insignificance. (*Montgomery v. Board of Retirement*, 33 Cal. App. 3d 447, 452, 109 Cal. Rptr. 181, 185, 1973)

The Illinois Supreme Court reached a similar conclusion in *In re Estate of Brooks* (32 Ill. 2d 361, 205 N.E.2d 435, 1965). A patient refused to accept a medically necessary blood transfusion because it violated her religious beliefs; her doctor and several attorneys for the state sought and obtained the appointment of a public conservator in order to override her refusal. On appeal, the court reversed the conservatorship orders, finding that the judicial attempt to determine what was best for the patient could not be "constitutionally countenanced" (32 Ill. 2d at 373, 205 N.E.2d at 442).

> Even though we may consider appellant's beliefs unwise, foolish or ridiculous, in the absence of an overriding danger to society we may not permit interference therewith in the form of a conservatorship established in the waning hours of her life for the sole purpose of compelling her to accept medical treatment forbidden by her religious principles, and previously refused by her with full knowledge of the probable consequences. (*Id.*)

The implication of these rulings and of *Sherbert* is that adults may endanger themselves if they so choose and if nothing injurious happens to anyone else. If state interest is not sufficiently compelling to override religiously motivated failure to receive medical treatment, then neither can state interest extend to interference with persons voluntarily choosing to engage in activities harmful to themselves by virtue of membership in a religious group. If they choose to fast or to live on low-protein diets or to go without sleep, they are entitled to do so.

> '[C]ompelling state interest' is conclusory in nature: the court will not find a compelling state interest—nor allow the state to prevail—until it has concluded that the state's interest is sufficiently compelling to *outweigh* the religious interest. Particularly in the close cases—those pitting a sincere religious belief against a compelling state interest—the compelling interest should not prevail when no harm to third parties can be shown. (Note, 53 N.Y.U. L. Rev. at 1278, emphasis in original)

Many of the new religious groups are indeed demanding of their adherents; that may well enhance their appeal, given balancing factors such as the varied services adherents feel the groups provide for them under one roof (see Robbins, 1981). The *Katz* appellate judge stated explicitly that the Unification Church members asking to be relieved of the conservatorships imposed on them had done nothing to injure or harm the legitimate interests of others. Thus the court could find no compelling state interest important enough to deny their petition for relief. Simply preventing a person from putting himself in danger cannot justify the imposition of a conservatorship. On the other hand, the *Katz* opinion implied that if the believers had become "gravely disabled" because of their religious activities, then the conservatorship requests of their parents might have been viewed in a different light (73 Cal. App. 3d at 989, 141 Cal. Rptr. at 256).

Even though the *Katz* case was decided by an intermediate California court, the opinion has carried considerable precedential weight. The questions before the courts in cases involving the new religious movements have been sharpened accordingly. Religious beliefs cannot be examined for their truth or falsity, so no religious belief can be used as a basis for assessing mental impairment or for imposition of involuntary civil commitment by way of conservatorships. "Nor can religious beliefs trigger a finding of 'dangerousness,' for religious faith as such poses no direct or immediate danger" (Shapiro: 770–71). Religiously motivated self-endangerment, moreover, is protected from state intrusion unless grave disabilities are incurred by believers. *Katz* boils down to the fact that the state could not make out its case that the five Moonists were in some physical or psychical way gravely disabled as a consequence of their activities in the Unification Church. Therefore, the remote possibility is left open that coercion or "mind control," if factually proven, could provide legitimate grounds for state intervention on behalf of parents attempting to de-convert their children from their new beliefs and to reroute them on their former ways of life. Focused in precisely this way, the most important of the new religious movement cases turn on the coercive persuasion, mind control, or brainwashing issues. These are matters of fact and evidence, not of hypothetical speculation by distraught parents or even of psychiatric evaluation by experts unless there be reasonable unanimity among them. (This the *Katz* case typically failed to provide, because the conflicting psychiatric testimonies simply cancelled each other out.)

The legal significance of the issue of mind control lies in its bearing on sincerity and on the genuineness of religious freedom. Clearly, if beliefs are coerced, then the value of freedom as protected by the first amendment is undercut, and sincerity as required by the *Sherbert-Yoder* test becomes questionable. Leaving to one side the much easier evidentiary matter of grave physical harm, the far more compelling tangle of problems associated with alleged cultic brainwashing must be faced. To the extent that legal decisions may involve regulation of religious belief apart from actions ensuing from belief, constitutional innovation could well be in store. Evidentiary consideration of mind control leads directly to inquiries about people's intrapsychic convictions. If inquiry is permitted in contravention of the venerable legal tradition that beliefs are inviolable and absolutely sancrosanct, then a new step toward the therapeutic state may also be in the offing. Of course that prospect chills civil libertarians; perceiving imminent danger, the American Civil Liberties Union has stoutly defended rights of new religious movement members in countless cases.

Exactly what the danger is requires precise rendering, for the interrelated questions at stake are exceedingly difficult to sort out. For the sake of argument, suppose that brainwashing and coercive persuasion techniques developed in POW camps have in fact been used on a person: these might include involuntary isolation, physical mistreatment, totalistic milieu control, shaming, debilitation and exhaustion, anxiety and despair, and false elimination of ambiguity (Schein: 321–27; Lifton: 419–37; and Davis: 441–50). Suppose further that the person's conversion or acquisition of beliefs resulted directly from the brainwashing process. A separable question still remains: does the individual now have the capacity to maintain himself in his belief? Or does the mind control under which he suffers amount to total volitional incapacitation?

Sincerity is another distinguishable issue. A person's conversion experiences relate to whether the new beliefs were voluntarily or involuntarily acquired; these circumstances, however, are logically independent of the sincerity of belief. A sincere belief may be held voluntarily or involuntarily, and the capacity to affirm it in the present context is conceivably different from capacities in play at the time of conversion.

Still another variable is that a person may voluntarily consent to a process of coercive influence with reasonable knowledge about what he is getting into. One may freely choose entrance into a coercive order. If informed consent holds up under inquiry, the person is competent regardless of mind control techniques employed on him. Otherwise an individual's freely committing himself to a religious system that involves discipline and obedience would be unintelligible (Shapiro: 789). An individual subjected to mind control, furthermore, might consciously and voluntarily decide to maintain himself in a continuing passive and submissive role vis-a-vis group leaders (controllers). This kind of decision, while perhaps distasteful to parents and courts, does not demonstrate incapacity. The presence of involuntary coercive persuasion does not conclusively prove present incompetence (*id.* at 790–91). In a conservatorship proceeding such as the *Katz* case, the burden should be on the parental petitioners to prove both mind control through coercive persuasion at the time of conversion, and present incapability of the person to control his own mind by virtue of abnegation to the will of another.

> [A]dherents who 'subject their reason to the demands of faith,' [Kelley] and demonstrate the depth of their commitment by insisting upon their beliefs as ultimate concerns, should not find the intensity of their faith being used as proof of their incompetence. Otherwise, the fact of adherence to a particular faith could itself become evidence of mind control, and the only way to show control over one's mind would be to renounce one's religion. (Shapiro: 795)

Put in this light, the burden on those asking courts for conservatorships over religious believers is onerous. But as Justice Jackson put it in *Ballard*, that may be one price we have to pay for our constitutional guarantees— mental and spiritual poison is beyond the reach of the prosecutor.

Inquiries into consensuality are permissible only if the nature and content of religious belief are left alone. If mind control is alleged, care must be taken that, for example, a religious belief that God speaks through group leaders is not subject to evaluation at the same time. The *Katz* appellate court was sensitive to this point:

> Evidence was introduced of the actions of the proposed conservatees in changing their life style. When the court is asked to determine whether that change was induced by faith or by coercive persuasion is it not in turn investigating and questioning the validity of that faith? (73 Cal. App. 3d at 987, 141 Cal. Rptr. at 255)

Again, since sincerity is a separable issue from consensuality, care must be exercised lest permissible inquiries into sincerity encroach upon the content of a believer's convictions. Partly because making these requisite distinctions imposes extraordinarily difficult demands on courts, many observers fear judicial innovation in which belief itself may come under formerly impermissible scrutiny. Shapiro worries about a "torrent of litigation that may threaten judicial devotion to the absolute sanctity of religious belief" (752). Jeremiah Gutman considers any assertion that the state knows better than the individual which groups are all right to join to be an indefensible intrusion on private belief (1979–80:70). The older bogies of court prejudice, prevailing public opinion, and predilections in favor of majority rule (Burkholder: 31) also come up in the new religious movement cases, with the newer twist that belief itself is often the issue in focus, and not regulable actions ensuing from belief.

The original conservatorship orders granted by the superior court in *Katz* were based neither on a finding of coercive persuasion during conversion nor on a determination that at the time of the proceedings, the five proposed conservatees were incapable of freely assessing their own beliefs and deciding whether or not they wished to maintain membership in the Unification Church. Harms to third parties did not come up, and no illegal actions were at issue. The *Katz* superior court judge focused instead on the integrity and significance of the family. Because of *Reynolds v. United States* and other anti-Mormon polygamy decisions, the state's interest in the viability and sanctity of the family has substantial weight. But in *Katz*, judicial buttressing of this interest egregiously transgressed the constitutional freedoms of religion and of association of emancipated adults. The superior court judge cited the "binding thing" of parental love for children (73 Cal. App. 3d at 963 n. 8, 141 Cal. Rptr. at 240 n. 8) and let it go at that.

So what was really at stake were the beliefs of the proposed conservatees. Their parents considered the new beliefs abhorrent, and they succeeded in convincing the superior court judge that something needed to be done to get their children back on the right track. Despite a request from counsel for the conservatees, the judge specifically allowed deprogramming procedures to take place during the time prescribed for the temporary conservatorships. The private religious beliefs of adult members of society were the sole issue.

> [T]he state's motive was derived from disagreement with the sect members' religious beliefs. The concerns that prompted the cult members' parents to seek the aid of the state—indeed, the proffered basis for the conservatorship orders—was the adherence of the members to a religious faith that their parents and, evidently, the superior court found repugnant. (Note, 53 N.Y.U. L. Rev. at 1287–88)

Not only did the court's orders unconstitutionally establish religion by treating members of the Unification Church differently and disadvantageously, they did so by focusing on belief itself, not on actions, not on harms to others, and, for that matter, not even on coercive persuasion and mind control.

The five proposed conservatees in *Katz* held sincere beliefs. No one would deny that imposing conservatorships on them constituted a severe infringement on their freedom to practice the religion of their choice. Specific harms were not proved, so the state's interest was not compelling. And conservatorships were hardly the least restrictive alternative available to the court because of the especially vulnerable situation that a conservatee must endure: even the safeguards that civil commitment processes must observe are bypassed. All the questions posed by the *Sherbert-Yoder* balancing test (see Chapter 1) were therefore answered in favor of the five Unification Church members. The appellate court, in clear recognition of the relevant constitutional circumstances, saw that the state could not support the parental petitions. The state cannot tamper with religious beliefs.

> Whatever the state may do to restrict the conduct of religious cultists, government actions aimed directly at altering a person's inner religious awareness are flatly proscribed. (Shapiro: 776)

"Pure beliefs" are the focus in *Katz* (see Weiss): whatever public display they may involve, they are nevertheless private, intrapsychic beliefs that do not impinge on the freedoms of others. And the conservatees requested neither specific permission to pursue a religiously defined goal in violation of a state regulation nor special religious exemption from a state requirement. The state had no grounds to find in favor of the parents.

> If conservatorships are upheld as a legitimate weapon with which to combat unconventional religious beliefs and practices, the courts will be setting off a series of unjustifiable investigations, accusations, and prosecutions that will go on without a

> foreseeable end, jeopardizing the atmosphere of free discussion of, adherence to, and dissent from religious views that the free exercise clause was designed to protect. (Note, 53 N.Y.U. L. Rev. at 1289)

Although the conservatorship cases are the most significant constitutionally, many other kinds of cases involving the new religious movements have been litigated. These groups frequently become embroiled in divisive land use and zoning controversies—for example, the Rajneesh in Antelope, Oregon, and the Scientologists in Clearwater, Florida. Internal Revenue Service cases also abound: the recent conviction and sentencing of Reverend Moon for tax evasion is only the most well-publicized instance. The Immigration and Naturalization Service has instigated countless cases against alleged illegal aliens. One important solicitation case took a position different from *Cantwell v. Connecticut* (see Chapter 1) by restricting members of the International Society for Krishna Consciousness to specified booths if they wanted to continue soliciting funds at a state fair. The Supreme Court ruled that this "booth restriction" was a reasonable place and manner restriction on the disruption that proselytizing and solicitation can cause at state fairs (*Heffron v. International Society for Krishna Consciousness, Inc.*, 452 U.S. 640, 654, 1981). The applicability of the holding should be limited to situations such as state fairs, where operation from booths is the norm. More open circumstances, such as airports, should not be affected by the *Heffron* decision.

Finally, in *Larson v. Valente* (456 U.S. 228, 1982), the Supreme Court invalidated a Minnesota statute imposing registration and reporting requirements on only those religious groups that gain more than fifty percent of their incomes from non-members—for example, from solicitation of outsiders. The action had been brought by members of the Unification Church, who sought a declaration that the statute was unconstitutional on its face and as applied to them. Justice Brennan wrote for the plurality of the Court. He took on all the hard issues because it was apparent to him that the first amendment establishment clause would have been severely undermined if the Minnesota law were allowed to stand. The free exercise clause was at stake, too, because the rights of members of novel or fringe minority sects would have been abridged by the Minnesota statute. Solicitation, after all, is legal even though the more established religious bodies need not rely on it so heavily as a new religious group.

> Free exercise thus can be guaranteed only when legislators—and voters—are required to accord to their own religions the very same treatment given to small, new, or unpopular denominations. (*Id.* at 245)

But the Court's holding in favor of the Unification Church members was predicated on the establishment clause's prohibition of denominational preferences.

> Since *Everson v. Board of Education*, 330 U.S. 1, 67 S.Ct. 504, 91 L.Ed. 711 (1947), this Court has adhered to the principle, clearly manifested in the history and logic of the Establishment Clause, that no State can 'pass laws which aid one religion' or that 'prefer one religion over another.' *Id.*, at 15, 67 S.Ct., at 511. This principle of denominational neutrality has been restated on many occasions. In *Zorach v. Clauson*, 343 U.S. 306, 72 S.Ct. 679, 96 L.Ed. 954 (1952), we said that 'The government must be neutral when it comes to competition between sects.' *Id.*, at 314, 72 S.Ct., at 684. In *Epperson v. Arkansas*, 393 U.S. 97, 89 S.Ct. 266, 21 L.Ed.2d 228 (1968), we stated unambiguously that 'The First Amendment mandates governmental neutrality between religion and religion. . . . The State may not adopt programs or practices . . . which "aid or oppose" any religion. . . . This prohibition is absolute.' *Id.* at 104, 106, 89 S.Ct., at 270, 271, citing *Abington School District v . Schempp*, 374 U.S. 203, 225, 83 S.Ct. 1560, 1573, 10 L.Ed.2d 844 (1963). And Justice Goldberg cogently articulated the relationship between the Establishment Clause and the Free Exercise Clause when he said that 'The fullest realization of true religious liberty requires that government . . . effect no favoritism among sects . . . and that it work deterrence of no religious belief.' *Abington School District*, 374 U.S. at 305, 83 S.Ct., at 1615. In short, when we are presented with a state law granting a denominational preference, our precedents demand that we treat the law as suspect and that we apply strict scrutiny in adjudging its constitutionality. (456 U.S. at 246)

Justice Brennan particularly concentrated on the establishment clause prohibition against excessive governmental entanglement with religion. He quoted from Chief Justice Burger's opinion in *Lemon v. Kurtzman* (see Chapter 1):

> 'This kind of state inspection and evaluation of the religious context of a religious organization is fraught with the sort of entanglement that the Constitution forbids. It is a relationship pregnant with dangers of excessive government direction . . . of churches.' (456 U.S. at 255, quoting from 403 U.S. at 620)

Brennan examined the legislative history of the Minnesota fifty percent rule and observed that the legislature had discussed "the characteristics of various sects with a view towards 'religious gerrymandering' . . ." (456 U.S. at 255). He concluded that the Minnesota rule was "not closely fitted to the furtherance of any compelling governmental interest" and that it set up "precisely the sort of denominational preference that the Framers of the First Amendment forbade" (*id.*).

It is both ironic and troublesome that Chief Justice Burger joined the dissenters in *Larson v. Valente*. In fact, only four justices subscribed to Brennan's opinion, with Justice Stevens concurring in the result. Led by Justice Rehnquist, the four dissenting justices challenged the standing of the Unification Church members to bring the action. Moreover, the dissenters objected to Justice Brennan's conclusion that the Unification Church was a "religious organization," since the lower courts had never ruled on the issue (456 U.S. at 267).

One wonders with some trepidation what the fate of cases like *Larson* will be after the retirements of Justices Brennan and Marshall. The Court is surely moving in an ominous direction for civil and religious liberties, partly under the leadership of Justice Rehnquist. He denies, for example, that the provisions of the first amendment are incorporated and made binding on the states by the fourteenth (see Fiss and Krauthammer: 14–21).

There is an interesting tactical side to this turn of events in the high Court. While it was almost always in the interests of civil libertarian lawyers to appeal civil rights cases to the Warren Court, today's litigants often find it to their advantage to go no higher than the circuit courts of appeal, which are fortuitously staffed by a large number of Carter appointees. So far the Court has declined to review the deprogramming cases that have come before it, but whether that trend will continue is anyone's guess.

Chapter 3
The Legality of Heresy

The most powerful voice that has been raised in support of judicial regulation of the new religious movement groups belongs to Richard Delgado, Professor of Law at the University of California at Los Angeles. He has exhaustively and ingeniously spelled out every conceivable ground on which the state could establish an interest compelling enough to justify infringing upon and controlling the new religions. His position, stated generally, is that the "cults" flourish only because of success at subjecting young people to regimes of totalistic control that can inflict deep harms on unsuspecting minds. Thus he argues that the state not only has the right but the humanitarian duty to protect its young by blocking cultic activities and by making it legally possible to extricate believers from their new commitments so that they may be restored to their former socially useful pursuits (see especially, 1977:62–72). Delgado's law review articles lay out a scholarly rationale for the quite common journalistic attacks on the new religious movements and for the anticult movement in general (on the latter see Shupe and Bromley). In theoretical perspective, his careful and comprehensive sequence of argumentation is an attempt to extend *parens patriae* doctrine by thinking about new religious movement devotees in medical terms.

Reliance on *parens patriae* authority to justify intervention into the lives of new religious movement adherents is riddled with legal and ethical problems. For example, psychiatric treatment of a person during a temporary conservatorship more often than not is undertaken without consent. Delgado nonetheless advocates deprogramming, a forcible intervention designed to rescue members of harmful religious groups: "deprogramming or other similar forms of confrontation therapy may well prove to be the only way certain victims can be retrieved from a state of mind control" (1977:85). He prefers state-authorized deprogramming to "self-help," which is "unadorned abduction," as opposed to "abduction under color of state law" (see Pritchard, 1978:3–21). Similarly, the Minnesota Supreme Court recently asserted that "owing to the threat that deprogramming poses to public order, we do not endorse self-help as a preferred alternative." But the court also implied that deprogramming under the auspices of state-sanctioned temporary guardianships would be acceptable, meeting the least restrictive requirement in a way that self-help does not (*Peterson v. Sorlien*, 299 N.W.2d 123, 129 and n. 2, Minn. 1980, discussed more fully in Chapter 9).

But even when carried out under conservatorship or guardianship orders, deprogramming is still enforced therapy or treatment, initiated (in most circumstances) without the volition or consent of the conservatee. Coleman and Solomon distinguish between volitional bona fide treatment and *parens patriae* treatment. For them the latter is unlawful—it is straightforward punishment, which without legal authority amounts to battery just as much as does an enforced surgical procedure (349 and n. 15). Benevolent intention on the part of professional therapists does not in itself result in bona fide treatment; only if the intended "patient" consents is psychiatric intervention genuinely treatment and not punishment. And of course neither treatment nor punishment for holding one sort of religious conviction as opposed to another is constitutional. Asserted right to treatment should not mask clearly illegal usurpation of authority, or a misuse of state *parens patriae* power.

> If . . . forced treatment is correctly termed punishment, a more honest term for right to treatment is *justification* for treatment. This label discloses the state's effort to rationalize, and to cast in the light of benevolence, its continuing punishment and control of deviants who might be difficult to process within the criminal justice system. The depiction of forced treatment as a right obfuscates the reality that the right to treatment is a justification for punishment. (Coleman and Solomon: 356, emphasis in original)

Delgado's response to this kind of argument is that nonconsensual therapeutic intervention performed on new religious movement group members is not punitive: it is restorative. It is not designed "to implant new values, impose a new set of loyalties, or compel the young person to become a compliant son or daughter" (1977:82). It is, accordingly, not like the original cultic brainwashing processes, even though Delgado admits that the procedures are often similar (see *id.* at 85 n. 444 on the methods of "lay deprogrammer" Ted Patrick). Furthermore, he argues that enforced therapy is not aimed at religious beliefs as such, but rather at "practices that are utilized to expand the numbers and powers of groups that happen to be religious" (*id.* at 84–85). He claims that first amendment doctrine presents "no insurmountable problems" (*id.* at 85); the issue is simply restoring free choice to persons impaired by membership in totalistic religious groups, thereby invoking benevolent *parens patriae* authority.

While Delgado's understanding of this point is surely subject to debate in ethical and political contexts, the thesis for present purposes is that it is also legally questionable (see LeMoult, *passim*, for cases and discussion, and the remarks in Chapter 2 on free choice). The confrontation between the *Katz* superior and appellate courts revolved precisely around this perception of *parens patriae* authority. The breed of benevolent paternalism espoused by Delgado was judged unconstitutional on first amendment grounds by the *Katz* court of appeal (73 Cal. App. 3d 983–89, 141 Cal. Rptr. 253–56). A person's religious commitments may not be used as grounds for the state to require him to prove his mental competence in order to avoid enforced therapeutic treatment. No determination of mental impairment may be based on religious adherence; legally, no one may be adjudged crazy by virtue of his faith. And even when the cluster of problems associated with involuntary acquisition of beliefs and present capacity to maintain them is introduced into the legal equation, grave doubt still hovers over anything like Delgado's argument. For at bottom, the mind control issues are matters of fact and proof; and "no court that has conducted an evidentiary hearing has found that any religious organization has subjected its adherents to mind control, coercive persuasion, or brainwashing" (Note, 53 N.Y.U. L. Rev. at 1281). Moreover, self-endangerment, by itself, is not a ground for state-authorized psychiatric intervention.

Professor Delgado bases another more recent argument for exercise of *parens patriae* power over the new religious movements on the thirteenth amendment's categorical prohibition of slavery. He avers that this approach has several estimable virtues. There is no need to balance interests under the *Sherbert-Yoder* test for protecting free exercise of religion. Assessing whether initial voluntariness is present at conversion is not required. The need for health and psychiatric evaluations to establish harms is obviated. And the whole issue of mind control and brainwashing is bypassed. If bondage and peonage could be shown on the basis of a group's living conditions or its authoritarian regimen, then the state has a clear avenue on which to intervene in order to extricate and "treat" members. The state is committed to these ameliorative thirteenth amendment thrusts—to preventing degradation of human personality and attendant misery and suffering, and to averting social ills such as megalomaniacal leaders and antipluralistic activities. If courts could objectively determine that religious groups are indeed carrying out peonage practices, then both criminal and civil remedies might become legally available, including the most drastic, physical removal of the "victim" via conservatorship orders (Delgado, 1979–80:51–67).

Delgado's thirteenth amendment analysis is merely another way to justify extension of the state's *parens patriae* authority. For him, the thirteenth amendment offers a more direct avenue for intervention in new religious movement activities than does the first amendment balancing of harms against free exercise rights. What is gained in directness and simplicity, however, may be illusory. Some policy decisions that we as a society may wish to make are constitutionally forbidden. Delgado recommends a thirteenth amendment approach that he thinks gets around the complicated first amendment issues discussed above. But the potential success of this end run seems questionable. For in new religious movement cases, assessing whether or not a condition of involuntary servitude indeed exists probably depends almost wholly on adoption of an external and critical vantage point.

> It is intuitively sounder to judge the conditions within these groups from the perspective of the outsider rather than that of the 'happy slave.' By our standards, and by those of ex-cult members, rank and file cult members live lives of misery and deprivation. (*Id.* at 61)

But constitutionally, the happy slave's rights are precisely what must be protected, even if as a consequence society must put up with more of Justice Jackson's mental and spiritual poison. People have the right to be miserable and deprived if they so choose. Roman Catholic monks and hermits are just as wretched "[b]y ordinary standards" (*id.*). If we leave it to the church to regulate them, so also must we leave it to the new religious groups to lay out a style of life for their adherents so long as they can continue to dig up converts by legal means. Peaceable persuasion, if not deceptive, is not by itself a coercive technique, and it is neither reasonable nor logical immediately to make the judgment that involuntariness must be in play or else people would not want to join a group whose beliefs and ways of living we find distasteful. To deny religious groups the right to proselytize is to sentence them to extinction, and that clearly cannot be done in the absence of a state interest compelling enough to override the guarantees of nonestablishment and free religious exercise.

Once again the thicket of claims and counterclaims about voluntariness must arise; however much we may wish to circumvent the issue, it is inescapable, and so consequently are the first amendment commands that have been considered here. Thirteenth amendment cases have been built on force, compulsion, and threat. If force or threat of force is involved in new religious movement conversion methods, "the question of whether one has voluntarily surrendered to a cult remains unresolved, and so we still must face the 'voluntary' issue which Professor Delgado claims we can avoid" (Gutman, 1979–80:69).

A thirteenth amendment rationale supporting governmental intervention may come a cropper precisely over the problem of happy slaves. Unless criminal acts are committed by group leaders to keep adherents in tow, then the state has no right to interfere. And if criminal behavior is going on, then its perpetrators are subject to criminal prosecution. We are left with the very same distinctions raised by cases weighing first amendment liberties against state interests. If fraud, or kidnapping, or deception can be proved, then the state not only has a defensible interest but also an obligation to prosecute. And if believers have been involuntarily reduced to "states of zombielike obedience" (Delgado, 1979–80:71) by virtue of coercive persuasion techniques, then the state may have the right and even the duty to rescue them so long as they are genuinely incapacitated. The same messy questions remain. Clear violations of the law must be prosecuted; but establishing whether a new religious movement member's state of mind provides evidence that laws have indeed been violated, or that values underlying our constitutional prohibition of slavery have been transgressed, is a task that the prosecutor must not undertake lightly (see Anthony).

Finally, all supporters of *parens patriae* regulation of the new religions—even on the thirteenth amendment ground that Delgado has recently espoused—see pathology and mental impairment in people's choosing to join and to maintain membership in these groups. Delgado's own convolutions on this point confirm this conclusion. He claims that his new approach avoids the "medical model" for legal purposes, yet in the very next breath he continues to speak of "cultist brainwashing" (1979–80:55). Conservatorships, moreover, still loom for him as an available remedy in cases "of persons who have fallen under the domination of cult leaders and whose psychological freedom has been demonstrably impaired" (*id.* at 65). "Impaired psychological freedom" and "zombie-like obedience" and "brainwashing" are merely other terms for pathology and mental disorder. Once involuntary behavior is imputed to someone, the disease or medical model is already in play.

> To the extent that 'sick' persons are the victims of inner pathological processes which interfere with normal behavioral functions, their behavior is assumed to be beyond their control. (Robbins and Anthony, 1982:285)

Supporters of *parens patriae* intervention argue that the person cannot help what he does; he is a victim of pathological compulsion, robbed of free will, in need of rescue and treatment.

Again, the asserted right to treatment of new religious group adherents may be a dangerous ploy that wrongly circumvents civil liberties and first amendment protections. To treat and cure, to restore freedom of choice and former life-patterns: these seem to be admirable goals on the surface, yet exercising benevolent *parens patriae* authority with respect to the new religious movements is simply one more link in the chain of evolution toward the therapeutic state (Kittrie, *passim*). A therapeutic vision of governmental services and sanctions leads to a debatable discussion of policy, and there may be legitimate considerations, for example, favoring treatment of convicted criminals rather than moral judgment and overt forms of punishment. But the more this vision is put into practice, the more deeply the question of "who is sick" presses. The more extensive state paternalism becomes, the more deviant and minority (but harmless) behaviors may be scrutinized, and the more people may have to fear from state-imposed, involuntary treatment. Thinking in medical terms about deviance feeds the growth of the therapeutic state, which seeks to coerce the maintenance of optimal mental health in all its citizens (see generally Robbins and Anthony, 1982). Where new religious group members are the deviants, compulsory psychiatric care is often the goal motivating alienated parents who try to get conservatorship orders from sympathetic courts. But this, for a civil libertarian such as Gutman, is nothing else than the "'Sovietization of medicine'" (quoted in Shupe and Bromley, 1980:224).

Consideration of the therapeutic revolution is intertwined with the profoundly antagonistic feelings that people often have about new totalistic and authoritarian religious groups. The state's therapeutic apparatus and its medical way of thinking about deviance give anticult citizens a way of stigmatizing cult membership as sickness. Rescuing "victims" is a laudable objective, and rescuers (vigilantes?) need not therefore be overly concerned with the niceties of civil liberties. "If cultism is *essentially* a medical issue it cannot also be a civil liberties issue, for the sick must be healed" (Robbins and Anthony, 1982:286, emphasis in original). The problem is that vigilante self-help rescue attempts, kidnapping, and forcible deprogramming are illegal. The *Katz* appellate court concluded that legal conservatorships for deprogramming purposes are also illegal in the absence of proof that lawless grave abuses are going on. No one disagrees that new religious movement illegalities should be subject to all state sanctions. Focusing on unlawful activity rather than on putative pathology within these groups would be a step in the proper direction. For it is nonverbal, intrapsychic behaviors, as opposed to criminal conduct, that bring constitutional concerns into play. Since *Sherbert* and *Yoder*, these concerns are weighted in favor of individuals' free exercise rights and against state *parens patriae* power.

We may wish for open-minded and tolerant people, but we cannot produce them through legal processes, for the rights of a person to be intolerant and dogmatic and narrow and servile are protected. Abuses of the law may be regulated and prosecuted.

> [But] problems arising from the power and authority wielded by cults over converts should be conceptualized as conflicts of authority between religious movements and other institutions, notably the state and the family. (Robbins, 1979–80:46)

Psychiatric afflictions may of course arise, but religious deviance is not necessarily and by definition a front on which state-condoned compulsory psychiatry may move. When we use the rhetoric of mental illness to justify intervention, we may both mask and exacerbate tensions within society that make new religious group membership look attractive in the first place and fuel the righteous vehemence of the anticult movement (Robbins and Anthony, 1982; Shupe and Bromley, 1980). And by stigmatizing new religious movements we may force members into further closure and further alienation ("deviance amplification") (Robbins, 1979–80:48).

If the focus of judicial attention shifts from cultic religious conduct regulable by secular interests toward the absolutely protected area of sheer belief, then a novel constitutional confrontation could lie ahead. Some courts have clearly seen this danger in recent years and have recoiled from it, as did the *Katz* appellate court. Prevailing public prejudices and popular medical stigmatization of the new religious groups ought not to lure courts into an unlawful concentration on individuals' internal states of mind and their private religious convictions. Seizing on the mind control issue in order to vault over required substantive findings and procedural safeguards could well lead to an unconstitutional expansion of the scope of judicial intervention (Robbins, 1979–80:38).

Religious beliefs by themselves were wrongly at stake in the original *Katz* proceedings (Note, 53 N.Y.U. L. Rev. at 1255 n. 53). A similar misplaced focus resulted in a New York grand jury indictment of leaders of the International Society for Krishna Consciousness. But a judge granted the defendants' subsequent motion for dismissal of the indictments, recognizing the clear distinction between criminal acts subject to the prosecutor's reach and spurious allegations of mind control put forward in order to justify state intervention. He found no legal foundation for the state's argument that religious activities and beliefs of the group constituted brainwashing, destruction of free will, or subjection of victims to unlawful imprisonment. He issued a caveat to prosecutorial agencies:

> [T]he premise posed by the People . . . is fraught with danger in its potential for utilization in the suppression—if not outright destruction—of our citizens' right to pursue, join and practice the religion of their choice, free from a government created, controlled or dominated religion, as such right is inviolately protected under the First Amendment. . . . (*People v. Murphy*, 98 Misc.2d 235, 413 N.Y.S.2d 540, 543–44, 1977)

Proselytizing and living under strict regimes of belief maintenance are not crimes. Neither is heavy indoctrination (413 N.Y.S.2d at 545). All these may involve mental and spiritual poison, and they may impede reasonable and logical thinking, but they are beyond legal recourse on the part of those who find them abhorrent. Religious freedom, to be sure, is the freedom to pursue, join, and practice a religion; and it is also the freedom to define one's own religious experiences and to associate with those who may see reality through similar lenses. Heresy is not subject to the prosecutor's reach.

PART II

Some Legal Foundations of Individual Rights

Chapter 4
The Context

Skirmishes continue between various outposts of the anticult groups and the new religious movements. The anticult contingent is highly organized and well funded (Shupe and Bromley, 1980: *passim*, and Richardson, 1977: *passim*); and the new religious movements may have increased enrollment even after Jonestown (*e.g.*, Hall: 16,19). It is not possible to give accurate figures about the magnitude of this continuing series of often painful confrontations, because the anticult groups are in the business of exaggerating the menace they see, and the new religions themselves sometimes make inflated estimates of their memberships. A recent *San Francisco Chronicle* story uses as fact the Citizens' Freedom Foundation claim that more than three million young adults are currently involved in some three thousand "destructive cults" (Hall: 16). But unless we know what is being taken as a "destructive cult" (Transcendental Meditation, Erhard Seminars Training?), such a count is meaningless. Scholars as opposed to journalists are far more subdued about numbers involved, and therefore about the extent of the "problem" (see, *e.g.*, Bromley and Shupe). But even if only a small portion of the American populace partakes of these various new religious movement wares, the impact of those who do so on the media is great, probably wildly disproportionate to actual indulgence. The impact is great because the stakes on both sides are of lively human interest: in the dramatic cult-related run-ins that have occurred for a long time now, parental concern bolsters asserted rights to restore adult progeny to a normal life, free from the totalistic fetters of whatever new guru happens to be on the block. By contrast, cultic devotees strenuously insist on their first and fourteenth amendment rights to believe and practice the religions of their choice, free from what they regard as outrageous and misguided stabs at domination and control by bereft parents. Obviously issues both of real freedom as well as possibly erroneous perceptions of unfreedom count strongly in the encounters daily chronicled by the press. Thus accusations of brainwashing on one side are matched in volume only by counter-accusations of the same thing on the other (see L. Coleman, 1982).

Forcible deprogramming—pictorially accompanied in the local press by all the predictably lurid details about kidnappings, hoodlums, muggings, motel rooms, irreparable harm, faked recantations, escapes—occupies center stage as the most vivid (and salable) of the procult versus anticult skirmishes. The pain, despair, and damage perpetrated by these incidents are surely real both to parents and their "cultically victimized" offspring; the latter agree about victimization but quite naturally see it as induced by their parents' decision to enter upon the course of involuntary deprogramming. These things really do not happen often, but if we were to count up the known cases from a period now more than a decade old, the number of people involved is likely sizeable. And although coercive deprogramming is only one sort of conflict between those favorably disposed to the rights of religious minorities on the one hand, and those so impressed by the dangers of the cultic menace in our midst that they resort to vigilante justice on the other, involuntary deconversion remains the most highly visible and emotionally charged point of confrontation. Thoughtful and knowledgeable people representing polar positions have joined this controversy. What the real issues are, however, is not as clear.

Just as it is not possible to provide accurate figures documenting the magnitude of the "cult problem," neither is it possible to say much that is genuinely telling about public opinion and its influence on this particular rift in American life. Anticultic views dominate the media, as movies such as "Ticket to Heaven" and a check of AP and UPI dispatches for any given period of time would attest. And this is true not only of the very popular media, but also of reasonably well-respected synthesizers of the latest in scientific developments such as *Psychology Today* and *Science Digest*. But reporting on media bias does not tell us how people really feel about these issues, for, patriotically, Americans also respond favorably when the Bill of Rights is touted. So we are witnessing deep conflicts in American life at a peculiar "crisscross" superimposed on all the other "grids" that divide the allegiances of Americans along ethnic, economic, class, and cultural lines (Cuddihy: 162–211). Conflicts raised by cults are deep because for the most part they are not decided in a knee-jerk, group- or status-related fashion. Major lines of cleavage may come within individuals or between individuals. Within individuals, numerous, often flatly contradictory, allegiances pull simultaneously, creating cross-pressures (J. Coleman: 47) that cannot be resolved by party or class or other group identification. Coercive deprogramming is surely one such line of cleavage, complicated further by rumor, gossip, and atrocity-story talk (Shupe and Bromley, 1981). Healing and academic professionals are as deeply divided as the lay populace in America. So are lawyers—some are active deprogrammers, some strong civil libertarians. What the society at large needs in order to make considered judgments is balanced analysis of correct information.

Research reports on already-formed opinions really do no good in this context. But what may help is an assessment of where the issue stands legally—how a society of individuals governed by a body of complex laws gains purchase on a deeply divisive set of conflicts. To make judgments about rights on each side, we need to know what those rights are. The law itself and careful reasoning about the law can aid in driving out prejudice, or at least in minimizing it as a basis for judgments, opinions, education and action. Innumerable civil and criminal actions spanning the last ten years have bound coercive deprogramming to legal adjudication. These cases pose the clearest point of conflict between rights claimed by religious adherents to believe what they wish, and rights claimed by parents to rescue alleged victims of corrupt and power-hungry authority figures bent on bilking and exploiting their faithful.

There are, of course, other hot spots of related conflict in the case law. Rights pertaining to solicitation, immigration, taxing power, zoning, municipal authority, and administrative law have been addressed in many different kinds of litigation. (See, for example, the conflict between the Food and Drug Administration and Scientology's claims about the curative powers of its E-Meter: *Founding Church of Scientology v. United States*, 409 F.2d 1146, D.C. Cir. 1969). Legislatures furthermore persist in considering various means of restricting cultic activities (see Gutman, 1983). But no new religious movement cases call forth such deep feelings or marshal such ideological extremes as do those involving coercive deprogramming. Far more important, no other kinds of new religious movement cases match in constitutional significance those featuring involuntary deconversion.

The force of this point would be diminished if confusions about these cases did not abound, if the rights claimed on both sides did not seem prima facie compelling, and if the legal issues under consideration were not so intrinsically delicate and arguable. Indeed, civil libertarian lawyer Jeremiah Gutman says flatly,

> Few other than constitutional lawyers realize what an integrated and intricate bit of business the First Amendment is. All of its intricacies are involved in the deprogramming issue. (1977:211)

Why confusions arise is no mystery: we are dealing with two hundred years of complex constitutional interpretation. No Supreme Court opinion on a deprogramming case yet provides guidance to the lower courts, and so conflicting views simply stand side by side. There is a modicum of agreement at this writing between three federal circuit courts of appeal in factually similar deprogramming cases (*Rankin, Ward* and *Taylor* discussed in Chapter 9 below). A further complicating factor is that federal statutes are directly involved in forcible deconversion cases, and the statutes in turn raise thorny judicial questions concerning constitutional sources of congressional authority. All this, finally, brings to the fore historical problems about the original intentions of the framers both of constitutional amendments and of implementing federal statutes. In sum, reliance on extraordinarily extensive and controverted legal scholarship is mandatory for understanding and for persuasive interpretation. (On constitutional hermeneutics, see Dworkin, 1979).

The sets of interpretative structures surrounding the first and fourteenth amendments are by far the most important means of gaining leverage on the legal status of deprogramming. But the fourth, fifth, eighth, thirteenth, and fifteenth amendments are also implicated more or less directly. The first amendment provides that Congress cannot prohibit the free exercise of religion, and that it cannot establish a religion. Despite attempts at stretching by some lawyers, the establishment clause does not mean that courts are forbidden to decide what is religious and what is non-religious for all kinds of purposes, including taxation, zoning, solicitation, and municipal authority. What the establishment clause does mean is that legislatures and courts cannot prefer one religion over another, or discriminate among religions. Religions, to be sure, can be regulated. But regulation, as we have seen, requires evidence of a compelling state interest, which must be balanced against the equal rights of any religion to coexist and practice freely in America along with all others. No religion, old or new, may be even tacitly approved by the legislative, judicial or executive branches. And the rights of religions must be protected in fully equal measure—public officials may not blink the rights of any religious group members, for example, by colluding in the kidnapping of a Moonie or a Love Israel member. Simply because these are the cases that tend to come up because of parental opposition, state officials must neither take actions nor avoid actions that they might take if older or "established" religions were involved instead. In deprogramming cases the free exercise and establishment clauses of the first amendment are always implicated: the right to be free from interference in religious exercise and the absolute injunction against the state's preferring one religion over another.

Congress may not, continues the first amendment, abridge freedoms of speech or the press. Again subject to ever-controverted regulation, Americans are free to speak and publish, read and hear (Gutman, 1977: 212 and Cox, 1981, *passim*). Activities such as disseminating literature, chanting and peaceful persuasion are therefore protected. Neither may the state interfere with the right to assembly—in deprogramming cases, this clause of the first amendment is contravened if persons are restrained against their wills from consorting with their religious brethren. And finally, the first amendment guarantees the right of people to petition government for redress of grievances.

> Even this right is denied by the deprogrammers and their confederates. When kidnap victims go to the police and seek arrest and prosecution of their tormentors and assailants, they find themselves at best the object of ridicule and rejection and at

worst arrested as material witnesses to their own alleged kidnappings, not by persons they accuse, but by their coreligionists, with whom they wish to be and from whom they have in fact been kidnapped. (Gutman, 1977:213)

The fourth amendment provides for security of persons and property against unreasonable searches and seizures, and the fifth, among other things, due process guarantees of security of life, liberty, and property. In Gutman's scenario, the relevance of the fifth amendment arises when, put dramatically:

A kidnap victim goes to the prosecutor to ask that her abductor be arrested and tried for kidnapping. Her abductor is not only not charged, although confessing the crime, but becomes a state witness against the victim's friends, accused of unlawfully imprisoning her by the heretofore undisclosed crime of brainwashing or mind control. The victim denies that any such thing happened, only to be met by the allegation that her denial of the event proves the efficacy of the control exercised over her mind. She is then placed in bail at an amount impossible to meet so that she can be available as a material witness to a crime she denies occurred. What has happened is that by connivance of the prosecutor she has been held, without indictment, without due process of law, and without the right to counsel for what the prosecutor has been told by the deprogrammers is the infamous crime of adherence to a religion of insufficient American antecedence to qualify for First Amendment protection. (*Id.* at 215)

A less vivid recital of events would make the same point: Americans under the fifth amendment do not have to be witnesses against themselves, and their liberty is guaranteed unless indictments satisfy constitutional requirements. Similarly, the eighth amendment protects against excessive bail, excessive fines, and cruel and unusual punishments.

In new religious movement cases, the thirteenth amendment's proscription on slavery comes up in two ways. The first concerns Delgado's somewhat hypothetical involuntary servitude argument, discussed in Chapter 3. Thus if it could be established that cult members were being held in servitude against their free choice, arguably the thirteenth amendment could be brought into play in a prosecutor's decision to indict group leaders. The second way in which the thirteenth amendment is implicated has to do with a congressional source of authority to punish private conspiracies, and will be addressed in greater detail in Chapters 7, 8 and 9. Cases of deprivation of voting rights bring the fifteenth amendment into consideration for similar reasons.

Finally, the fourteenth amendment is crucial because of its privileges and immunities, due process, and equal protection clauses. Section 1's broad language provides:

> No State shall make or enforce any law which shall abridge the privileges or immunities of citizens of the United States; nor shall any State deprive any person of life, liberty, or property, without due process of law; nor deny to any person within its jurisdiction the equal protection of the laws.

This casts a large penumbra indeed, and deprogrammed plaintiffs often appeal to it, but its remedial value frequently has been questioned over the years. Everything hangs on judicial interpretation of section 5 of the fourteenth amendment: "The Congress shall have power to enforce, by appropriate legislation, the provisions of this article." Unfortunately, the enforcement clause also raises complex and highly controversial issues on which the courts are divided; theories about the fourteenth amendment as a source of authority for remedying tortious conduct and interpretative case law will be analyzed in what follows.

New religious movement constitutional litigation, more than scholarship or journalism, lays bare the conflicts generated between distraught parents and the anticult movements on one side and minority religions and their adherents on the other. These cases and the conflicts they present are far more significant than the small number of Americans directly involved suggests. Constitutional decisions enhancing (or curtailing) religious liberty may be in the offing as a result; moreover, other crucial issues such as the role of psychiatry in the courtroom are being raised and adjudicated. The consequences of judicial determinations undoubtedly will not be wholly satisfying either to anticultists or to civil libertarians. The Supreme Court is not likely to make clear-cut decisions on all fronts, and the lower courts probably will continue to split. Careful legal analysis can reduce blinders of misinformation and prejudice. Legal scholarship has no more vital role than to educate the profession and the public about what is actually occurring in courtrooms and about the social ramifications of legal decisions. All Americans are affected—not just the parties to particular cases. Since the "cult problem" is not going to fade from the scene in a short period of time, judicial decisions, particularly at higher court levels, will become increasingly significant factors in the conflict.

Legal issues will continue to arise because people see abuses on both sides, from one vantage point, in the recruiting and retention policies of new religious movements, and from the other, in the vigilante methods often used by parents and their hired agents forcibly to remove adults from what they perceive as harmful and wrongful cultic allegiances. The antagonists trade coercive persuasion charges. And as we saw earlier, some observers question the utility of the coercive persuasion concept when ripped from its original context, thought reform and prisoner of war camps complete with real bondage and real barbed wire.

The active anticult movement, as well as much of the public, the media, and concerned scholars, wish for effective intervention into the affairs of new religious groups. They claim that deceptive and excessively high pressure forms of recruitment constitute constitutionally viable grounds on which to interfere with and curtail at least some of the most flagrant abuses. Professor Delgado makes the following observations concerning the claim of critics of new religious movements ("destructive cults"):

> Full membership means subjection to a totalistic regimen, a highly controlled lifestyle, and identification of the group with the forces of good and the outside world with the forces of evil. It means disidentification with parents, career plans, former friends and family and immersion in the cult and its goals—principally raising money and converting new members. Critics charge that cultists suffer a loss of autonomy and decisional capacity, are bilked of their money and property, and suffer physical and psychological impairment as a result of medical inattention and extreme stress.
>
> These factual allegations are asserted either to be true of the religious group's general practices, thus warranting a broad-scale remedy, or true in particular cases, justifying relief with respect to a particular member or members. The religious groups either deny these charges, assert that the violations occur at most in isolated cases, or defend by saying that their practices are constitutionally protected, and are no different from those of other social groups. Some defenders of the groups urge that the allegations are really masks for religious intolerance and are aimed at new groups because they think, act, and dress differently from the rest of us. Still others say that even if charges of physical and mental devastation are true, these effects are incurred by competent adults, choosing voluntarily, and hence are beyond the state's purview. (1981:2–3)

Delgado here recognizes that when constitutional issues arise, we are not dealing with a simple pro- versus anticult polarization. Different slants of view are more subtle than that and are always colored by one's own philosophical, ideological and religious stances. For example, it is not a bare "procult" position to defend the civil liberties of all religions equally strongly, for someone taking that position could be quite thoroughly convinced that grave abuses are indeed occurring in new religious movements as well as in older ones. Such a person might find all religious goings-on abhorrent, yet defend other people's rights to pursue them. Similarly, vehement anticultists might be pure secularists or, for instance, right-wing evangelical pentecostalists whose own version of Christian orthodoxy is threatened by the Moonies or by the New Testament Missionary Fellowship. Since all shades of opinion are represented, and many different rationales and justifications are advanced, the pro- and anticult shorthand we all use greatly oversimplifies divisions among us.

Full consciousness of this phenomenon is required as we turn attention to the constitutional problems and innovations that have been brought about by new religious movement litigation.

The remainder of Part II deals with, in order, a theory of the affirmative power of the state to confer freedom under the aegis of the fourteenth amendment and a theory regarding the nature of human rights provided for in the American Constitution. These theories are based on the work of the jurisprudential philosopher Ronald Dworkin and the legal scholar Archibald Cox. I do not wish to defend their theories here, but rather to use them as benchmarks for understanding the case law and constitutional questions I shall be discussing. Chapter 6 analyzes the Ku Klux Klan Act of 1871. The Act, now codified in part at 42 U.S.C. section 1985(3), is a Reconstruction period legislative attempt to enforce the fourteenth amendment's equality-of-rights language. In Chapter 7, I follow the fate of the Klan Act, which lay relatively dormant as a weapon for enforcement of rights for nearly one hundred years. Chapter 8 examines the impact of the Supreme Court's decision in *Griffin v. Breckenridge* (403 U.S. 88, 1971), which paved the way for the revitalization of the Klan Act as an avenue of redress for those harmed by private conspiracies aimed at depriving groups of citizens of their entitled rights.

Chapter 5
The Constitutional Rights of Individuals

The line of cases that provides the precedential background for decisions in recent civil deprogramming litigation goes back to the Reconstruction era. Interpretation of these cases is technical and subject to dispute. But legal commentators agree that one's interpretation of this line of precedent determines one's view of the viability of forcible deconversion suits brought by new religious group members against their deprogrammers and, often, against their parents, relatives, and friends as well. Constitutionally, considerations that non-lawyers might think quite important for deciding deprogramming cases, for example, the special nature of parent-child ties, are largely irrelevant, more telling for the emotional atmosphere in which a case is heard than for its legal determination. Of course sometimes courts blink constitutional niceties, as the *Katz* superior court did, only to be overruled by an appellate court sensitive to the rights of the proposed conservatees.

Since so much rides on the way we are going to understand the constitutional rights of individuals, it seems wise to suggest a vantage point: a theory of rights as they are imbedded in the Bill of Rights and later amendments to the Constitution, as they have been implemented and clarified by the legislative branch, and as they have been interpreted by the judiciary. This is not the place to defend any one theory exhaustively. But some philosophical considerations will serve to illuminate the significance of much that follows, and will help to keep the central issues in view in analyzing the technical legal background to the involuntary deprogramming cases.

Until well into the twentieth century, the Supreme Court applied a rights-privileges distinction on many fronts trenching on constitutional law. It was understood that privileges were bestowed by government, while rights had solid constitutional and historical common law sources. Privileges could be withheld by government; rights could not. This distinction no longer washes cleanly. The realm of privileges has receded and that of rights has been expanded by recent interpretation because the withholding of privileges has come to be perceived as violating constitutional rights. Much of the reason for this shift is rooted in growing dependence of the public on the government in providing for the poor. But the government, in fairness, could not foster reliance by proferring benefits, then withdraw them as mere privileges. So the Court developed the doctrine of "entitlements," interests not founded on constitutional claims of right but on expectations raised by the state in its citizens.

> While these new 'statutory entitlements' did not grant a constitutional right to governmental non-arbitrariness whenever benefits were being provided (since government remained free to foster *no* expectations in distributing its largesse), they did serve to surround the 'core' of liberty and property interests with a periphery activated, unlike the core, only by affirmative state choices, but secure, once activated, against destruction without due process of law. (Tribe: 515, emphasis in original)

Interestingly, *Sherbert v. Verner* (see Chapter 1) was one of the landmark cases contributing to the demise of a rights-privileges distinction. According to the Court, Mrs. Sherbert's claim to receive unemployment compensation could not be dismissed on the ground that unemployment benefits are mere privileges rather than rights. "It is too late in the day to doubt that the liberties of religion and expression may be infringed by the denial of or placing of conditions upon a benefit or privilege" (374 U.S. at 404). The Court buttressed the point in a note by referring to cases in which conditions and qualifications for governmental benefits had been struck down because of "their tendency to inhibit constitutionally protected activity" (*id.* at 404–5 n. 6).

The Court's evolving theoretical perspective on individual rights has swallowed up the earlier rights-privileges distinction. So fundamental rights now are exercised in a more expansive constitutional framework than before. But what are "fundamental rights" in our constitutional system in the first place? Not wholly arbitrarily, the idea of equality presents itself at the beginning. The Declaration of Independence proclaims:

> We hold these truths to be self-evident, that all men are created equal, that they are endowed by their Creator with certain unalienable Rights, that among these are Life, Liberty and the pursuit of Happiness.

Rights enumerated here are explicitly dependent on the framers' conception of a natural ("self-evident") claim to equality. The equal protection clause of the fourteenth amendment is quite clearly not the only legal justification for the right of citizens to seek equal treatment under the laws, for the due process clause of the fifth amendment has also been relied upon, as well as the Bill of Rights taken as a whole. And commitment to equality of treatment really underlies the entire Constitution, not just sections of it read literally (Tribe: 992). However indirectly, this view of the Constitution reflects the moral universalism that Thomas Jefferson wrote into the beginning of the Declaration of Independence (Pole: 53–58).

Egalitarian principles upon which the American constitutional polity was founded were natural in the sense of ultimate for the framers. They relied on a Lockean notion that civil laws secured the laws of nature but did not supersede them. As legal historian J. R. Pole observes:

> The function of civil law was rather to give security to existing natural rights by establishing forms and procedures. Just government could come into existence only by the consent of those who voluntarily entered into it, and who lived under it, for the protection of rights already recognised by natural law. (8)

Of course in actual practice a moral universalism of natural rights at first produced merely a property-owning aristocracy; only much later and quite gradually has "equality of rights" developed into genuine equal opportunity, and early natural rights rhetoric turned into a genuine avenue of social expectation in America (Pole: 129, 136). What has made that change possible is "the perception that equality must itself be the result of social choice, effected by private or political decisions" (Pole: 354). Equality, we see now, is a right hard-won, not an inalienable God-given one. But it is still a right possessed by individuals antecedent of legislation or convention (see Dworkin, 1977:176):

> [I]t is the individual whose rights are the object of the special solicitude of the Constitution and for whose protection the Republic had originally justified its claim to independent existence. (Pole: 358)

The deprogramming cases in Chapter 9 dramatize another step in the long constitutional process aimed at securing the right of equality in voting, access to public facilities, education, and housing. These cases extend judicial affirmations of equality beyond the confines of racial concerns to those of religious minorities. Although the rights to free exercise of religious belief and freedom from religious establishment are immediately at stake, it is the Republic's commitment to equality that makes the new advances in religious liberty possible. Were it not for the struggles attendant upon obtaining civil rights for racial minorities, constitutional precedent for expanding the rights of individuals in socially scorned new religious movements would be lacking.

In the law, further precision about equality is required. We can speak of the right to equal treatment, understanding by that the right of every citizen to have the same access to a specific interest, say, the vote, as every other. More broadly, we may also speak of the right to treatment as an equal, which "holds with regard to all interests and requires government to treat each individual with equal regard as a person" (Tribe: 993). Thus political and judicial decisions cannot be prejudicially based. Prejudice comes into play in various ways. Invidious discriminations by government deny the right of individuals in basically similar circumstances to treatment as an equal (for example, length-of-residence rules for voting and racial eligibility for public school attendance). Vice-versa, failure to make requisite discriminations among those differently situated can also deny right to equal regard (for example, mandatory flag-saluting regardless of religious persuasion, mandatory voting in person regardless of handicap or sickness or travel, or mandatory payment of school bus fees regardless of financial ability to do so). Invidious governmental classifications contribute to *de jure* discrimination, denying equal regard; governmental failure to classify may, on the other hand, produce *de facto* discrimination, also compromising equal regard. The latter is a far more thorny constitutional issue because it involves determining whether the government has affirmative duties to redress disadvantages or injuries that arise apart from state action (Tribe: 993–94 and nn. 18 and 20). Cases of deprogrammed plaintiffs seeking remedies against parents and deprogrammers usually, though not always, fall into this category, and it is no surprise that lower courts are divided as a result.

The coercive deconversion cases would not be so hard for judges and juries to decide if we were all clearer about the primacy of the right to treatment as an equal. Religious liberty is less at stake in these cases than, as Dworkin puts it, the right to "equal concern and respect" of the law (1977:180–205 and *passim* and Rawls, *passim*). Speaking generally, the key constitutional right is equality, and basic liberties depend on it, not the other way around. The right to a distinct liberty, such as religious free exercise, demands recognition only when the fundamental right to treatment as an equal can be shown to require it (Dworkin, 1977: 273–74).

> [T]he right to distinct liberties does not conflict with any supposed competing right to equality, but on the contrary follows from a conception of equality conceded to be more fundamental. (*Id.* at 274)

Rights to liberties are surely constitutionally vital to individuals, but they do not involve blanket license. No one may claim a right to be utterly free from constraints (Berlin: negative liberty), so liberty as license is most often not the real issue when cases arise featuring fundamental freedoms guaranteed in the Constitution.

> If we have a right to basic liberties not because they are cases in which the commodity of liberty is somehow especially at stake, but because an assault on basic liberties injures us or demeans us in some way that goes beyond its impact on liberty, then what we have a right to is not liberty at all, but to the values or interests or standing that this particular constraint defeats. (Dworkin, 1977: 271)

The "standing" in question, then, is each individual's right to treatment as an equal. In turn that standing demands that we apply strictest scrutiny to government-sponsored deprivations of liberty, particularly those justified on expediential policy grounds (for example, governmental security pitted against reporters' first amendment rights). Similarly, we must be attuned to deprivations of liberty that occur *de facto*. Treatment as an equal is also vitiated if the government takes no action to forestall or deter deprivations of fundamental liberties even where no direct state action is alleged (for example, private conspiracies engaged in racial discrimination or in vigilante justice—see the following chapters).

A primary emphasis on the right to equal concern and respect of the law, or on the right to treatment as an equal, squarely confronts utilitarian rationalizations. It is often thought that conflicts between individuals and the state must always be subject to a balancing-of-interests procedure of the sort articulated in *Sherbert* and *Yoder* for religious concerns. But even where such weighings do take place, the courts are not necessarily or always committed to balancing off fundamental rights of individuals against some conception of the common good, as if equivalent values were implicated. Fundamental rights rather take precedence over social policies or perceived advances in social circumstances of the polity. Following the right-based theories of Rawls and Dworkin, the point is that individual rights must be served even if the general welfare may be harmed in some way as a consequence (Dworkin, *id.* at 173 and see generally 150–83). Put another way, the Constitution and the amendments discussed above shield the individual against majoritarianism. In Dworkin's words:

> The Constitution, and particularly the Bill of Rights, is designed to protect individual citizens and groups against certain decisions that a majority of citizens might want to make, even when that majority acts in what it takes to be the general or common interest. (*Id.* at 133)

The right to free expression, for example, is a right that citizens hold against the government. A clear majority might think that preventing certain sorts of speech would benefit society as a whole; but the state cannot negate free speech on these utilitarian grounds alone, for that would be to undermine the constitutional presumption of the primacy of fundamental rights. Dworkin argues:

> The existence of rights against the Government would be jeopardized if the Government were able to defeat such a right by appealing to the right of a democratic majority to work its will. A right against the Government must be a right to do something even when the majority thinks it would be wrong to do it, and even when the majority would be worse off for having it done. (*Id.* at 194)

This is a moral argument. Or, precisely, it is an argument that the fundamental rights protected by the Constitution were moral rights antecedent to their having been forged into legal rights of citizens. Rights like freedom of worship and freedom of expression, and perhaps implied rights such as privacy, cannot therefore be transgressed by governmental fiat on grounds of utilitarian gain. Dworkin makes the same point by distinguishing between principles and policies. Principles secure the fundamental rights of individuals or groups. Policies are designed to advance some collective goal of the community (*id*. at 82). Principles may not be transgressed in favor of policies, even where the majority agrees that society would be improved by doing so. Perceived gains in the common weal do not suffice to override rights, that are, in principle, fundamental. The due process and equal protection clauses of the fourteenth amendment are vague and difficult to apply because they do not provide specific recipes; rather they appeal to moral concepts.

Treatment as an equal is chief among the fundamental rights incorporated into our most vital constitutional amendments (Dworkin, at 136–49). Whatever balance is struck between individual interests based on the right to equal regard, and interests of the state based on the goal of maximizing social benefit, must be weighted in favor of the individual. (See Cox, 1981, for an analysis of recent Burger Court attempts to adjudicate between government interests and the right to free expression guaranteed by the first amendment). Governmental concerns do not compete directly with personal rights; they are not equivalent. The exercise of rights may of course cause inconveniences, even actual affronts to a clear majority (as, for example, in pornography cases). But inconvenience or affront cannot provide arguments for prohibiting what a right allows or allowing what a right protects against. Fundamental rights, particularly the right to treatment as an equal, safeguard what Dworkin calls both human dignity and political equality: in the Constitution a moral vision of human equality becomes the set of political rights protecting the weak against the strong, or minorities against majorities. Even clear gains for the majority's preferences cannot justify abridgment of these rights.

> [I]f rights make sense at all, then the invasion of a relatively important right must be a very serious matter. It means treating a man as less than a man, or as less worthy of concern than other men. The institution of rights rests on the conviction that this is a grave injustice, and that it is worth paying the incremental cost in social policy or efficiency that is necessary to prevent it. But then it must be wrong to say that inflating rights is as serious as invading them. If the Government errs on the side of the individual, then it simply pays a little more in social efficiency than it has to pay; it pays a little more, that is, of the same coin that it has already decided must be spent. But if it errs against the

individual it inflicts an insult upon him that, by its own reckoning, it is worth a great deal of that coin to avoid. (Dworkin, 1977:199)

These ideas do not simply trade on pious sentiment; our constitutional system is in fact committed to them. But what if more than majoritarian preferences or marginal benefits to society are at stake? What if state interests of the most vital sort seem to be threatened by an individual's choice to play out what appears to him to be a right protected by the Constitution? What if a reporter's publication of government secrets would seriously undermine American intelligence operations, perhaps costing the lives of officers who were exposed as a result? Cases testing these kinds of conflicts come up regularly. The Pentagon Papers case against Daniel Ellsberg, the *Progressive*'s publication of alleged hydrogen bomb construction classified data, and the government's accusations against ex-CIA agent Frank Snepp for the publication of *Decent Interval* are recent examples of conflict between the right to freedom of expression and asserted national security interests (see Cox's discussion, 1981:5–14).

Under right-based theory, every dire emergency situation society faces must be clearly demonstrable in order to warrant breach of rights; the emergency may not be merely hypothetical. Failure to obey a law most often does not constitute a genuine crisis, nor does failure by the state to enforce all laws. Since fundamental constitutional rights are not just legal, but rather antecedently moral, it is hardly surprising that cases often arise involving individuals who claim a moral right to break a specific law. The arguments in confrontations like these must be examined with care: the right thing to do in the circumstances may well be the wrong thing to do under a given statute (for example, forms of civil disobedience). But if government, in defense of its interests, asserts that rights may be suppressed in the face of an emergency, it must demonstrate what will happen if a right is acted upon, and not just what it thinks might happen. "If we allow speculation to support the justification of emergency or decisive benefit, then, again, we have annihilated rights" (Dworkin, 1977:195). Oliver Wendell Holmes' famous dictum about clear and present danger ("and the danger . . . one of magnitude") is apposite here (*id.*).

The issue of speculation justifying violation of rights because of some alleged imminent threat to society is closely linked to the role that prejudice can play in forming policy decisions conflicting with rights. Prejudicial scare tactics overly inflate common projections of some awful tear in the social fabric if individuals are permitted to exercise their constitutional rights. Integrated schools and forced busing to insure them look to some observers like devastating blows to the American way of life (civil rights); so does publication of forbidden materials (freedom of expression) and court-sanctioned permission to abort (right to privacy). All of our fundamental rights, when actually played out in the public arena, sometimes appear deeply threatening to others, perhaps even to the majority of citizens. When conflicts like these occur, many are willing to override rights in order to maintain what they view as an already-established and vital social policy (segregated schools, for example). Conversely, they are willing to override rights in order to cancel what are perceived as dangerously novel policies (rights to contraceptive devices, abortion, or possession of pornographic materials, among others).

Coercive deprogramming cases afford extraordinarily dramatic instances of the link between unjustified speculation about emergency and untutored prejudice. Since the role popular media play in the establishment of opinion about new religious movements is so great, a broad avenue devoted to purveying a skewed view of "the cults" has become extremely well-trafficked. Media reportage about minority religious groups is heavily couched in prejudical lingo.

> That which we would destroy, we first label pejoratively: A religion becomes a cult; proselytizing becomes brainwashing; persuasion becomes propaganda; missionaries become subversive agents; retreats, monasteries, and convents become prisons; holy ritual becomes bizarre conduct; religious observance becomes aberrant behavior; devotion and meditation become psychopathic trances. (Gutman, 1977:210)

Pejorative terms like these have dominated newspaper, magazine and television accounts of Moonies and Hare Krishnas for over a decade, and of course the overwhelming tragedy of Jonestown exacerbated already-irresistible tendencies among journalists to trade on such inflammatory language.

The media's tendency to trot out atrocity stories and anecdotal evidence drawn from successfully deprogrammed apostates increases its already powerful influence over public opinion.

> Coercive deprogrammings had a number of effects on the fortunes of the new religions. Foremost was their immediate discrediting through the media by the production of apostates of the new religions. A number of coercively deprogrammed ex-'cult' members engaged in face-saving attempts to account for their period of membership in these deviant groups, and, prompted by deprogrammers (who had an interest in portraying themselves as valid 'liberators' of a pernicious captivity) as well as parents (who also sought an extraordinary explanation of their offspring's questing in unconventional groups, yet wanted to avoid marking them with any permanent stigma), they recounted a fairly standard litany of horrors ranging from claims that they were manipulatively recruited and brainwashed into 'cults' to various tales of deliberate family estrangement, deceptive fund-raising, and political conspiracy or illegal lobbying. By telling such stories, apostates absolved their families as well as themselves for any

responsibility for their errant behavior and paid the price of contrition, thereby reentering the previously rejected community. Thus, the stories not only resolved the families' problem of explaining offsprings' deviance, but through their 'smoking gun' quality as eye-witness evidence they seriously discredited many new religions. . . . Overall, the single and most important effect of deprogramming was the creation of the apostate role and accompanying atrocity stories. (Shupe and Bromley, 1980:166)

Thus the media are constructing an emergency situation, namely the victimization of our children by totalistic minority religious groups. That can only feed flames of prejudice that were, unsurprisingly, rekindled by Jonestown.

Dworkin defines prejudice in a precise and helpful way. Prejudices are postures of judgment that rely on considerations that are or ought to be excluded by our conventions (1977:249). Trials, for example, are structured by rules defining what constitutes reliable evidence; prejudicial hearsay may not be admitted. More generally,

Our conventions stipulate some ground rules of moral judgment which obtain even apart from such special contexts, the most important of which is that a man must not be held morally inferior on the basis of some physical, racial, or other characteristic he cannot help having. (*Id.* at 249–50)

Varied and complex factors of background, rearing, and contemporary influence combine to produce prejudice in an individual, denying equal concern and respect for another of a different race or ethnic group, or of a different sexual or religious persuasion. Good reasons or justifications for holding such views are, nearly by definition, lacking. Sheer emotional knee-jerk reaction (phobia or obsession); rationalizations based on erroneous factual understanding, say, about racial inferiority; or "parroting" arguments of the "everyone knows that" sort: these, alone or in combination, rather than good and discussable reasons are the sinews of prejudice (*id.* at 250). They cancel a claim to hold a moral position. We can generalize about majority opinion in society, but that is not necessarily to strike a point about a genuine moral position, for prejudice rather than reason often underlies opinions of a democratic majority. Fear and abhorrence of some novel religious phenomena may rest on rationalizations, unsupported assumptions of fact, and on vague perceptions of threat to the family, established religions, and the shared religious assumptions of the Republic (Shepherd, 1978: *passim*).

[T]he principles of democracy we follow do not call for the enforcement of the consensus, for the belief that prejudices, personal aversions and rationalizations do not justify restricting another's freedom itself occupies a critical and fundamental position in our popular morality. (Dworkin, 1977:254)

Moral positions grounded in reason are enforceable by law; prejudices grounded in feeling are not. Thus policies directed toward commonly despised small religious groups must be based on reasoned principles of individual rights rather than on the community's emotional aversion, even when that aversion is widely shared.

The argument that it is hard to find real conflicts between general welfare and treatment of everyone as an equal (Miller: 387–91) will not wash in the face of cases that have arisen from anticult hostility unleashed upon adult members of new minority religious movements. When state officials are directly involved in depriving freedom and the right to unfettered religious exercise—as for example, when police openly aid deprogrammers in kidnapping and restraining a new religious group member—then the stricture that the state may not treat groups differently comes into play. Discrimination among groups, reflecting parental preferences and subjecting members of only some groups to tacitly sanctioned illegal acts, is precisely what the Constitution protects against. There can be no establishment of religion and all are guaranteed the pursuit of religious truths according to their own lights. The antecedent or "natural" right to treatment as an equal is hence secured in theory, although endlessly difficult to be assured in practice.

Constitutionally, though, these present the easier cases. What happens if, wholly apart from state action or state sanction, parents and their hired agents band together in conspiracy to rob cultic adherents of their rightful religious liberties, and to treat them in an invidiously discriminatory way because their new views and allegiances are despised? Answering this question requires unraveling a maddeningly complex legal tangle, and the answer cannot be definitive because the courts are divided. And that is not the only reason. The answer to the question has been left hanging to some extent in the interstices between the judicial and legislative branches.

Put briefly, the Warren Court in several crucial decisions concerning individual constitutional rights issued Congress an invitation to secure tightly the right to be free of discrimination even when its source is private and does not involve color of state law or state action. By widening congressional powers of enforcement, particularly under the equal protection clause of the fourteenth amendment, the Court expressed the view that government has affirmative obligations to protect citizens against interference with their fundamental rights. Commenting on these cases, Archibald Cox remarks:

> The original Bill of Rights was essentially negative. It marked off a world of the spirit in which government should have no jurisdiction; it raised procedural barriers to unwarranted intrusion. It assumed, however, that in this realm the citizen had no claim upon government except to be let alone. Today, the political

> theory which acknowledges the duty of government to provide jobs, social security, medical care, and housing extends to the field of human rights and imposes an obligation to promote liberty, equality, and dignity. For a decade and a half recognition of this duty has been the most creative force in constitutional law. (1966:93)

The fourteenth amendment's essentially negative injunctions are the focal point of this extension. Thus even though section 1's prohibitions refer only to state actions, and not to those of private citizens, congressional power under section 5 to enforce the prohibitions may extend to the regulation of private activities because these activities encroach in varying degrees on whether privileges and immunities, rights to life, liberty, and property, and equal protection of the laws are in fact guaranteed to each citizen. In other words, the fourteenth amendment is read in a positive light: the state has the duty to protect against private actions that interfere with basic rights and liberties (Cox, at 102 and *passim*). On this reading, the fourteenth amendment secures the freedom and equality to which the Constitution is already committed; it does not simply lay negative injunctions on state power. The practical enjoyment of rights therefore is protected even against the private actions of other citizens if their effect is to deny treatment as equals to members of despised minorities.

Judicial activism and the interplay of power among the three branches of government are really the principal issues that lie behind the egalitarian thrust of the deprogramming cases. The problem parallels the recent history of desegregation in America. Congressional authority to root out the vestiges of segregation in schools and lunch counters was surely available but went unused because of successful obstructionist tactics by senators and representatives from the South. Executive leadership was not forthcoming. So the judiciary in its landmark education and public facility decisions acted to secure treatment as equals for blacks on the practical level, thereby eradicating further badges and incidents of slavery. As Archibald Cox argues,

> [T]he need for judicial action is strongest in the areas of the law where political processes prove inadequate, not from lack of legislative power but because the problem is neglected by politicians. (*Id.* at 122)

To be sure, an expansion of federal power is also required since enforcement of the fourteenth amendment's equal protection mandate falls to the Congress at the Court's recent invitation. Should Congress fail to respond, constitutional adjudication by the courts nevertheless has national and not just local implications.

Throughout the 1960s and early 1970s, judicial decisions laid the groundwork for the law to reach and punish private conspiracies that had the effect of denying treatment as an equal not only to racial minorities but to members of other despised groups as well. Commentators disagree about how these decisions should be interpreted. But precedents are clearly available to secure the rights of individuals implied by fourteenth amendment restrictions on state authority over citizens. Judicial activists have increasingly insisted that the states have affirmative duties correlative with these restrictions: states must act to ensure that rights are not abrogated in the private sphere just as they must maintain vigilance to avoid abridgment of rights engineered by state officials. Many sorts of cases have elicited this extension of national power, including those involving persons discriminated against and harmed because of their religious persuasions. But the cases involving discriminatory treatment of religious minorities are particularly important because nearly all of them draw upon both the first and the fourteenth amendments, as well as disputed implied rights such as rights to privacy and to travel.

If the state has an affirmative duty to prevent inequalities and harms stemming from invidious discrimination, the source of failure to afford treatment as an equal to all is irrelevant: private action as well as state involvement (or failure to become involved) must be regulable and punishable. And this is the direction in which recent constitutional adjudication has moved. The fourteenth amendment rights at stake have been delineated with ever greater specificity. Thus only recently have deprogrammed plaintiffs been afforded the ability under certain circumstances to maintain a constitutional cause of action (see Chapters 8 and 9). The rights in question are not vague rights against all the world. They are rather rights against particular persons or groups engaged in activities that have the practical effect of denying fundamental rights. States through their judicial authorities are therefore finally being required to carry out in practice the duties demanded by section 1 of the fourteenth amendment. As Cox observes:

> The Fourteenth Amendment says nothing of rights; it speaks only of duties and it lays duties only upon the State. The exactly correlative rights are to have the State perform its duties. (1968:65)

Freedom to choose and define one's own religious belief is clearly guaranteed by the first amendment to the Constitution and, less directly, in other binding passages. But even the most significant constitutional guarantees have never been automatically available. They must be won over and over as new challenges arise in varying circumstances. The deprogramming cases are important not only because they have brought forth a new way to secure old rights in practice, but also because they have built on recent precedent to expand and extend our whole idea of constitutional rights and the affirmative duties of the states with regard to them. This advance is unintelligible apart from its antecedence in the struggle for racial equality in this country. So we must step backward to focus on the roots of the struggle, bearing in mind Archibald Cox's now-famous remark: "Once loosed, the idea of Equality is not easily cabined" (1966:91).

Chapter 6
"An Act to Enforce the Provisions
of the Fourteenth Amendment to the Constitution"

Securing the rights of newly emancipated blacks in a practical way was a cardinal objective of the Reconstruction Congresses. For this reason, the thirteenth, fourteenth and fifteenth amendments were drafted and offered to the states; they were ratified in 1865, 1868 and 1870, respectively. Theoretically, of course, the rights enumerated in the Bill of Rights would have sufficed to do the job of implementing full citizenship for former slaves. But the circumstances were special, and obviously Jefferson's moral universalism had never been put to this particular test. The thirteenth amendment abolishing slavery, the fourteenth amendment guaranteeing privileges and immunities, due process, and equal protection of the laws, and the fifteenth amendment prohibiting denial or abridgment of the right to vote took long further steps toward realization of equal treatment for all Americans. More than a century later, that ideal has not been fully reached. Yet the Republic has come a considerable distance from the colonial period, in which rights were accorded primarily to land- and slave-owners.

Legal scholars dispute the original intention of the framers of the fourteenth amendment. Indeed, "theories of legislation" in general are disputed in American jurisprudence. If a statute enacted by Congress unambiguously specifies rights and duties and if it embodies a reasonable political goal, then few problems of interpretation arise because there is substantial agreement about new obligations to be enforced by the courts. Several factors must combine if a statute is to achieve unambiguous clarity. In older days, a preamble set forth the intent of the legislation, and the language became an official part of the new law itself. Sometimes now a committee report serves the same function, as do floor speeches of legislators who are acknowledged sponsors of a given bill. These factors, along with other more amorphous ingredients, such as dicta and opinion among debators of a bill, comprise the "legislative history" of a statute, what is often called by lawyers the "original understanding." Clarity and binding force of interpretation are further enhanced if good political arguments are available justifying policies or principles advanced by a new law.

Unfortunately, with some legislation no agreed-upon original intention stands out, no general collective understanding of a bill's aim finds consensus, and possible justifications collide. Then judges must make decisions one way or the other predicated on their own principles of political morality, recognizing that they are injecting substantive content that may or may not have been contemplated by the drafters of the legislation. Cases involving the fourteenth amendment and the 1871 Civil Rights Act designed to enforce it tend to fall in this latter category, and no important decisions have escaped argument based on differing readings of legislative history and on projections of various conceivable principles and policies. Conscious that it too is subject to debate, I shall present one general view here and raise objections to it as the cases present themselves. (On the jurisprudential issue of theory of legislation, see Dworkin, 1979:37–43.)

Constitutional amendments naturally carry more clout and enjoy far greater permanence than statutory enactments, but the problems of construing them are similar. Once the thirteenth amendment had been adopted, Congress moved to eradicate legal disabilities associated with involuntary servitude. The broad language assuring all citizens equal treatment and treatment as an equal in the fourteenth amendment gradually emerged from lengthy congressional disputation. During fourteenth amendment debates before the Joint Committee on Reconstruction, testimony about conditions in the South did not center on deprivation of rights spearheaded by state or governmental action. On the contrary,

> [t]he principal ingredient is a pervasive pattern of private wrongs, motivated by popular prejudice and hostility, directed against Negroes primarily and to a lesser, but significant, degree against Northern whites and against those Southern whites who had been disloyal to their states by being loyal to the Union. (Frantz: 1354)

Wrongs addressed by the committee were largely acts that would violate ordinary homicide and assault laws. But especially in the South, special circumstances required national attention in order to ensure enforcement of the laws. The Republicans ran in 1866 on a platform promoting the fourteenth amendment as a means of empowering Congress to deal with the horrors depicted to the committee. Long-time abolitionists in particular perceived the extraordinary damage that could be wreaked by private prejudice-driven hostility toward blacks when combined with states' failure to protect them. Republican strategy was to enhance the authority of Congress to redress the situation; it was not to bolster the power of the judiciary to reach abuses explicitly perpetrated or sanctioned by the state officials. The fundamental problem as the framers of the fourteenth amendment saw it lay in private wrongs systematically sheltered by state inaction (*id.* at 1356–57).

Following the ratification of the fifteenth amendment in 1870, the group of leaders that had been primarily responsible for the fourteenth amendment also shepherded through Congress several new pieces of enforcement legislation. Two of them were conspiracy statutes. The Enforcement Act of 1870 ("An Act to enforce the Right of Citizens of the United States to vote in the several States of this Union") mostly concerned the fifteenth amendment, but also the thirteenth because of the clear tie between race and illegal denial of the right to vote. Because state government officials were the target of the Enforcement Act, very little was made of the Act's private conspiracy language and its consequent linkage to the thirteenth amendment (see Buchanan: 334–36). The conspiracy section of the 1870 act is broad and appears almost out of place in legislation focused on eradicating limitations on voting rights. Section 6 made it a felony to conspire with others

> to injure, oppress, threaten, or intimidate any citizen with intent
> to prevent or hinder his free exercise and enjoyment of any right
> or privilege granted or secured to him by the Constitution or laws
> of the United States. (Current version at 18 U.S.C. section 241)

While this section of the Enforcement Act has been largely ignored until recently, its private conspiracy language was the heart of the Ku Klux Klan Act, passed the following year.

On April 20, 1871, Congress made into law "An act to enforce the Provisions of the Fourteenth Amendment to the Constitution of the United States and for other Purposes," known as the Ku Klux Klan Act (partially codified at 42 U.S.C. section 1985[3], Supp. V 1981). Since the Klan Act expressly reiterated the private conspiracy language of the Enforcement Act, there are two instances of congressional legislation aimed at regulating conduct of private citizens when the practical consequence of discrimination denies a minority the right to treatment as an equal. Regulation in the Enforcement Act took the form of a criminal statute. The Klan Act created a civil cause of action—a constitutional tort allowing victims of conspiratorial denial of rights to sue their tormentors. Despite the apparently plain phrasing of both acts, there is still considerable debate about the intent of their drafters. Some scholars (e.g. Avins: 1968) insist that the framers of these civil rights acts never intended them to enable Congress directly to reach private conspirators entirely apart from actions of state officials. It is true that Representative Bingham's original draft of section 1 of the fourteenth amendment, which was meant to give Congress direct positive power to enforce rights of citizens, was revised and essentially stricken. After criticism, Bingham redrafted the section to mirror article I, section 10 of the Constitution. The revision imposed negative limitations on state powers and superseded his original uniform law providing for punishment of any offenses against the life, liberty, or property of citizens. The kind of thinking that forced this redrafting may lie behind the Enforcement Act and, more arguably, the Klan Act as well: if the fourteenth amendment did not grant Congress express power to punish violations of legal rights by private parties, then legislation implementing the amendment would not do so either.

But solving this particular problem of interpretation unfortunately is not that easy. The Act of 1870, enforcing the fifteenth amendment, and that of 1871, enforcing the much broader fourteenth, both contain clear language outlawing conspiracies by individuals if denial of rights or of equal protection of the laws ensues. And many of their framers contended that proper enforcement of these two amendments required an increase in federal power so that Congress could reach acts of private conspirators. That is how the majority of Republican legislators seemed to read section 5 of the fourteenth amendment and section 2 of the fifteenth: Congress shall have power to enforce the provisions of these articles by appropriate legislation. Others, mostly Democrats, may have assumed that a state official must be involved in order to trigger congressional enforcement powers. These congressmen feared a drastic extension of federal control over both states and citizens and therefore urged strict limitations on national government interventions designed to secure voting, due process, and equal protection rights. For them, only violations obviously and actively implicating state officials could trigger federal remedial action.

Another factor in this clash of opinion had to do with the legacy of a fugitive slave case, *Prigg v. Pennsylvania* (41 U.S. 539, 1842). Justice Story had held in *Prigg* that the national government had direct power to enforce the fugitive slave clause contained in article IV, section 2 of the Constitution; for him this was a federal duty, one that had not been delegated to states. In fact, he argued that states could not be made to take over this national obligation (*id.* at 615–16). Under this construction, the federal government has more power over private individuals than it does over states or state authorities acting in their official capacities. The *Prigg* opinion had considerable influence for many years (Avins, 1968: 338–42), and the Enforcement and Klan Acts may have been written in its light. That would explain the clear language in both laws about federal responsibility over conspiracies denying rights of national citizenship. But still unresolved would hang the problem of the relationship between the enforcement acts and the fourteenth and fifteenth amendments, which place negative injunctions only on governments and say nothing at all about conduct of private citizens.

The steam pressuring this debate has not decreased in more than a hundred years. In fact it has intensified in the wake of several Supreme Court decisions expanding the sphere of federal prerogatives to protect against deprivation of rights (see, for example, *United States v. Guest*, 383 U.S. 745, 1966). As in all questions of constitutional interpretation, historical evidence about the framers' intentions is crucial. But here they seem almost contradictory. There is a disquieting logical gap between the language of the fourteenth and fifteenth amendments on the one hand, and legislative attempts to provide national enforcement of them on the other; yet the framers of both are pretty much the same group.

The issue is clear: either state involvement in civil rights violations is a prerequisite to federal intervention, or it is not. Courts and scholars have not resolved the issue and continue to disagree. The power of the national government would be enhanced if the courts expand upon recent Supreme Court advances in construing Reconstruction conspiracy legislation. Certain acts of private citizens, which before had lain only under the governance of the states, would instead come within the jurisdiction and punitive power of the federal courts. Many see this development as an unwarranted and overly entangling federal usurpation of authority over the private person. They assert that power to punish or otherwise deal with discriminatory and right-depriving conspiratorial actions should continue to lie with the states, lest the federal-state division of labor become severely skewed.

But this reading of the contemporary problem simply reproduces one side of the Reconstruction debates. What happens, asks the critic, when the states do not act, rights consequently continue to be violated, and injured citizens have no avenue of redress? Much of the 1871 congressional debate about the Ku Klux Klan Act centered on this question. Part of the act concerned deprivations of rights caused by state action. Since the fourteenth amendment explicitly forbade the states to deny equal privileges and immunities, due process, and equal protection, Congress had relatively little difficulty passing enforcement legislation creating a civil cause of action for redress (see 42 U.S.C. section 1983). But what has become for our purposes the more significant part of the Klan Act concerned a civil cause of action designed to allow injured individuals redress against other individuals conspiring in a wholly private pact:

> If two or more persons in any State or Territory conspire, or go in disguise on the highway or on the premises of another, for the purpose of depriving, either directly or indirectly, any person or class of persons of the equal protection of the laws, or of equal privileges and immunities under the laws, or for the purpose of preventing or hindering the constituted authorities of any State or Territory from giving or securing to all persons within such State or Territory the equal protection of the laws; . . . in any case of conspiracy set forth in this section, if one or more persons engaged therein do, or cause to be done, any act in furtherance of the object of such conspiracy, whereby another is injured in his person or property or deprived of having and exercising any right

or privilege of a citizen of the United States, the party so injured or deprived may have an action for the recovery of damages, occasioned by such injury or deprivation, against any one or more of the conspirators. (17 Stat. 13, 1871, now codified at 42 U.S.C. section 1985[3])

No mention at all of state action or color of state law appears here, and debates on this issue in the Forty-second Congress were accordingly more heated and more divisive than those on the state involvement section of the Klan Act. Although the language could not be clearer, argument about intent and construction was neither lacking at the time of passage, nor is it today. Supporters of the act realized full well that in practice the effects of privately engineered discrimination were just as harmful to victims as state-initiated hindrances placed in the way of fourteenth amendment guarantees. So they argued that the clear language of the private conspiracy section of the Klan Act meant what it said: Congress reaches exclusively private conspiracies to deny civil rights by creating a federal constitutional tort action giving victims potential monetary and injunctive relief against their tormentors.

The stance taken by supporters of the Klan Act reopened debates similar to those that had forced emendation of Bingham's original fourteenth amendment language from positive conferral of rights on all to negative injunctions placed on state action alone. Federal encroachment on states' duties was again a flash point, countered by Republicans' insistence that the national government must act to secure in practice rights granted in theory by the Constitution and its amendments. And again the *Prigg* doctrine that Congress has more direct authority over individuals than over the states figured in the debate—"the mere recognition of a right in the federal Constitution gives Congress implied power to protect it from interference by private acts" (Frantz: 1357). Arguing against those who perceived federal usurpation of duties left to the states, supporters of the Klan Act relied on section 5, the enforcement clause of the fourteenth amendment, as warrant for the claim that protection against abridgment of civil rights could fall to federal governance. Opinion at one pole held this duty of the national government to be virtually unlimited: federal action to secure rights could be prophylactic as well as remedial. Thus in order to act, federal authority need not await allegations of actual discriminatory denials of equal treatment by some citizens against others. Indeed, when construed literally, this is the thrust of section 1985(3), the private conspiracy portion of the Klan Act.

Democratic Party opponents, falling back on their earlier arguments against the thirteenth and fourteenth amendments, would have delimited federal power far more narrowly. Congress could correct or protect against deprivations of rights only when they were officially sponsored by state action. According to the opposition, granting the national government more jurisdiction over enforcement of rights would foster "such a vast expansion of congressional power as to wipe out the states" (Frantz: 1358). To this argument was closely linked opposition of the same coalition to direct federal sway over private wrongs ("Individuals alone cannot enslave"—remarks of Representative Blair, *Cong. Globe*, 42d Cong., 1st Sess., app. 208, 1871, quoted by Buchanan: 338). Since the target of the Klan Act was really a much broader range of conceivable affronts to citizens' rights to treatment as equals, this narrow construction could not carry the day. The Act of 1871 was, after all, supposed to enforce the all-encompassing privileges, immunities, and equal protection language of the fourteenth amendment. Even if these were read only as incidents of slavery to be overcome, the problem was still to implement a set of sweeping rights secured to all citizens, and, more particularly, to secure rights protected against private conspiratorial discrimination. Senator Edmunds remarked during the debates:

> Therefore when the prohibition against slavery was enacted and the power was expressly put into the hands of Congress to carry out that enactment, to see that it was made effectual, was it not the right and the duty of Congress, too, to the last point of its power, to protect the liberty of all people wherever it might be assailed by that form of crime? (*Cong. Globe*, 42d Cong., 1st Sess. 695, 1871, quoted by Buchanan: 338)

When passage of the Klan Act appeared imminent, an intermediate theory of its meaning began to present itself. This too was woven together from a series of assumptions that may or may not have been shared by all the framers and ratifiers of the proposed new law. Some legislators apparently thought that the rationale for the private conspiracy section of the Klan Act lay in states' systematic and willful failure to enforce fourteenth amendment obligations regarding treatment of citizens as equals. Therefore Congress was forced to act under its enforcement entitlement. For these legislators, a showing of antecedent state inaction was the triggering mechanism invoking federal protection of citizens against private conspiracies and punishment of conspirators. According to this view, victims of right-denying private conspiratorial activities could bring federal suit against conspirators only when states deliberately failed to protect them. Members of Congress who thought that the national government could act directly against invidiously discriminating conspiracies formed an alliance with the group supposing a prerequisite of antecedent state inaction. Although obviously their readings of the act differed considerably, together they constituted a clear majority over the bill's Democratic opponents, who still asserted the necessity of positive state discriminatory action before the federal government could act.

The distinction seems fine, perhaps even trivial. But it has telling relevance. Much of the 1871 congressional debate over whether state failure to act supplied sufficient color of law was quoted by both sides nearly a hundred years later in disputes centering around the Supreme Court's decisions in *United States v. Guest* (383 U.S. 745, 1966) and *United States v. Price* (383 U.S. 787, 1966). For example, Representative James Garfield, who became the ill-fated twentieth President, expressed as well as anyone the antecedent state inaction theory that ensured passage of the Klan Act.

> But the chief complaint is not that the laws of the State are unequal, but that even where the laws are just and equal on their face, yet, by a systematic maladministration of them, or a neglect or refusal to enforce their provisions, a portion of the people are denied equal protection under them. Whenever such a state of facts is clearly made out, I believe the last clause of the first section [of the fourteenth amendment] empowers Congress to step in and provide for doing justice to those persons who are thus denied equal protection. (*Cong. Globe*, 42d Cong., 1st sess., app. 153, 1871, quoted by Frantz: 1358–59)

The question then becomes, who is punished by the federal government, negligent state officials or the private parties to a conspiracy themselves? On a broad reading of the Klan Act, it is the latter; on a narrow construction, only the former. For over a century this question has been debated and has remained unsettled. It has come up frequently in the checkered history of the Klan Act, and only recently has a narrow construction given way to a broad and expansive rendering by the Supreme Court and by some lower courts.

While the antecedent state inaction theory permitted passage of the Klan Act, it clearly did not solve all the associated problems of interpretation. Because the assumptions and ideologies of its framers differed, it is difficult to specify their actual intentions with any precision. If the framers in fact understood that an action could be brought against conspirators only when the state failed to act, that understanding might have allayed fears of a drastically novel imbalance between federal and state power. But, on a literal reading, the targets of the conspiracy section were the conspirators themselves, and Congress thus would seem to have asserted authority directly to reach private acts of citizens. This leaves the negligence of state officials in limbo: if the framers understood that the act would reach only officials, they did not say so. What they did say is that victims of conspiratorial deprivation of rights may have a cause of action for recovery of damages against the conspirators.

Early Supreme Court interpretations of the Klan Act narrowly construed the act's reach, virtually nullifying the constitutional tort made available by the legislation (see Chapter 7). Broadening the construction of the act to conform to its express language has been a task left to courts a hundred years after its framing and passage. There is no question that the modern national government as a consequence has assumed jurisdiction once considered to be the domain of the states alone. So the older understanding of the federal-state balance of power has shifted, but as Cox (1966) argues, this is perhaps no more than a reflection of increasing federal responsibilities for welfare of citizens in almost all areas of contemporary life. Hammering home this plank in a legal structure designed to guarantee treatment as an equal to all citizens does not amount to a fearful federal encroachment. It is rather a logical extension of the struggle for equality that the Civil War was all about in the first place; the "nationalism of 1871" (Howe) is embodied not least in the Klan Act.

How the Klan Act has evolved into a means of advancing religious as well as racial liberty and equality is still another story. The 1871 debates were directed not only to the problems of congressional enforcement power and antecedent state inaction, but also to the correct understanding of the act's scope. Obviously, the legislation was aimed at overcoming badges of slavery and so arguably only at the amelioration of the legal and political condition of blacks on whom citizenship had been newly conferred. But the scope of the Klan Act differed from that of the Enforcement Act of 1870, which focused on eradicating racially imposed voting liabilities (fifteenth amendment). As legislation intended to enforce the fourteenth amendment, the Klan Act by its very nature had to be concerned with the whole gamut of rights specified there: privileges, immunities, due process and equal protection of the laws. The fifteenth amendment protects in precise terms the voting rights of former slaves. The fourteenth amendment, by contrast, is couched in vague and virtually all-encompassing language, including all and excluding none. So in the debates of the Forty-second Congress over the bill's scope, this question emerged: in addition to blacks, which if any minority groups could avail themselves of the federal cause of action for redress of right-denying conspiracies? Who, in other words, could count as a victim, and under what circumstances?

Because of pervasive concern among congressional leaders over the issue of illegitimate federalization of tort law, the language of the conspiracy section of the Klan Act had to be framed carefully. In fact, the parent of section 1985(3) evolved as an amendment from floor discussions in 1871. Modern courts have construed the act to cover instances of discriminatory motivation, that is, cases arising from conspiracies formed on the basis of animus toward members of a despised minority group. This reading is warranted by the legislative history of the bill even though express language about motivation and animus is lacking. Some limiting mechanism both was and is required, however. Otherwise the scope of the section would become far too sweeping, and any citizen theoretically could use it to redress grievances against any other. Tort law awarding damages for wrongful acts thus would become wholly and probably unconstitutionally federalized.

The framers of section 1985(3)'s predecessor therefore wanted the federal remedy to come into play only if no sufficient state cause of action were available, or if there were some good reason for a victim not to rely on state machinery. From debate centering on invidious prejudice-driven discrimination emerged the theory that a federal remedy for deprivation of constitutional rights ought to be available when special, perhaps only local, circumstances made appeal to state courts unsuitable. While of course Congressional leaders could have singled out a specific set of circumstances involving Southern blacks, they chose not to circumscribe the Klan Act that narrowly. So while the question of what sort of conspiracies might be drawn into the purview of the act was thoroughly discussed, it was not resolved. The legislative jockeying that occurred has become significant in subsequent judicial interpretations of the new law's reach.

Desire to nail the Ku Klux Klan for its terrorism against blacks provided the original impetus for fashioning a federal, constitutional tort remedy. But the conspiracy section of the Klan Act addressed a far more extensive tangle of ills, focused on majoritarian domination of minorities that compromised the rights of the latter to treatment as equals. This broader reading is supported by the legislative history of the section. Senator Hoar pushed the bill in order to ensure

> that under no temptation of party spirit, under no political excitement, under no jealousy of race or caste, will the majority either in numbers or strength in any State seek to deprive the remainder of the populace of their civil rights. (*Cong. Globe*, 42d Cong., 1st Sess. 335, 1871, quoted in Note, 64 Minn. L. Rev. at 645)

And Senator Edmund's remarks have been seized by later courts seeking to stretch the act to cover conspiracies not motivated by race:

> We do not undertake in this bill to interfere with what might be called a private conspiracy growing out of a neighborhood feud of one man or set of men against another to prevent one [from] getting an indictment in the State courts against men for burning down his barn; but, if in a case like this, it should appear that this conspiracy was formed against this man because he was a Democrat, if you please, or because he was a Catholic, or because he was a Methodist, or because he was a Vermonter . . . then this section could reach it. (*Cong. Globe*, 42d Cong., 1st Sess. 567, 1871, quoted in Note, 64 Minn. L. Rev. at 645)

Senator Edmund's comments were directed to Representative Willard's amendment, the parent of the conspiracy section of the Klan Act and of section 1985(3). Willard's objective was to limit the law's scope, given the broad original formulation. But as the Supreme Court subsequently declared in *Griffin v. Breckenridge* (403 U.S. 88, 1971):

> [T]he explanations of the added language centered entirely on the animus or motivation that would be required, and there was no suggestion whatever that liability would not be imposed for purely private conspiracies. (*Id.* at 100)

Representative Willard focused his justification of the amendment on equality:

> [T]he essence of the crime should consist in the intent to deprive a person of the equal protection of the laws and of equal privileges and immunities under the laws; . . . the Constitution secured . . . equality of rights and immunities, and . . . we could only punish by United States laws a denial of that equality. (*Cong. Globe*, 42d Cong., 1st Sess., app. 188, 1871, quoted in *Griffin v. Breckenridge*, 403 U .S. at 100)

According to Representative Shellabarger:

> The object of the amendment is . . . to confine the authority of this law to the prevention of deprivations which shall attack the equality of rights of American citizens; that any violation of the right, the *animus* and effect of which is to strike down the citizen, to the end that he may not enjoy equality of rights as contrasted with his and other citizens' rights, shall be within the scope of the remedies of this section. (*Cong. Globe*, 42d Cong., 1st Sess., 478, 1871, quoted in *Griffin v. Breckenridge*, 403 U.S. at 100)

Representative Shanks argued against amending the bill so as to remove its "frank assertion of the power of the national Government to protect life, liberty, and property, irrespective of the act of the State" (*Cong. Globe*, 42d Cong., 1st Sess., app. 141, 1871, quoted in *Griffin v. Breckenridge*, 403 U.S. at 101). Senator Pool and others insisted that Congress must deal with individuals, not states (403 U.S. at 101). No supporter disputed that minorities other than blacks would be protected under the act, as long as the requisite invidious discrimination and class-based animus in fact motivated wrongful denial of the right to equal concern and respect of the laws.

Modern courts have been seriously divided on criteria defining groups with sufficient shared characteristics that animus directed against their members may be treated as class-based. Answers have ranged from "discrete, insular, and immutable" minorities to the broad "sharing of an intellectual nexus." Sexual and religious discrimination counts. Traditionally disadvantaged groups carrying a history of adverse discrimination usually qualify, and there have been numerous less obvious candidates in a barrage of recent litigation. Courts that have heard cases brought by deprogrammed plaintiffs against their kidnappers under section 1985(3) have agreed that class-based discriminatory animus against members of new religious movements does indeed exist; and further that such animosity can motivate right-denying conspiracies between parents and their hired agents to deploy coercive deconversion procedures. Sufficient identifiable traits are shared by members of a given fringe religion that warrant exists for invoking a section 1985(3) remedy. These courts have generally agreed that prejudice similar to racial prejudice among members of the wider society often victimizes participants in despised minority religions. So members of these marginal groups do appear to have a cause of action for redress of deprivation of civil rights under the Klan Act.

The recent section 1985(3) rulings significantly enhance and extend the *Sherbert-Yoder* movement toward broadening the scope of first amendment religious liberty, as incorporated into and buttressed by the fourteenth amendment. But nearly a century of retraction and rescision of civil rights preceded the contemporary advances in protecting free religious exercise. And the Ku Klux Klan Act was among the Reconstruction measures temporarily eviscerated by the courts in apparent contradiction of the intentions of its framers.

Chapter 7
The Klan Act in the Courts

Sentiment fueling the drive of the Reconstruction Congresses to ensure equality under the laws held up only for a short period of time.

> In 1876 the structure of Reconstruction was already crumbling and its impending defeat was evident. In 1883 its defeat was a fact which the North had accepted and acquiesced in for six years. (Frantz: 1361–62)

The Supreme Court decisions in *United States v. Reese* (92 U.S. 214, 1876), *United States v. Cruikshank* (92 U.S. 542, 1876), *United States v. Harris* (106 U.S. 629, 1882), and the *Civil Rights Cases* (109 U.S. 3, 1883), bear witness to this unhappy initial period, turning aside and thwarting the clear intentions of the framers of the Reconstruction amendments and their enforcement statutes. This anti-Reconstructionist spirit proved to be malignantly hardy: it persisted until the Warren Court's activism in the opposite direction, revitalizing the post-Civil War drive toward securing *de facto* as well as *de jure* treatment as equals for all American citizens.

Received dogma has it that these Supreme Court decisions from 1876 to 1883 carry enormous precedential weight because they were the first and virtually contemporary judicial constructions of the civil rights amendments and statutes. That is not so. Earlier federal court determinations decisively carried forward the thrust toward national guarantees of equality made available by the Reconstruction era congresses. For example, in *United States v. Hall* (26 F. Cas. 79, C.C.S.D. Ala. 1871, No. 15,282), Judge Woods sustained an indictment brought under the Enforcement Act charging conspiratorial deprivation of rights. He confirmed congressional authority to protect the fundamental rights enumerated in the Bill of Rights, as extended and secured by the fourteenth amendment. Under the latter, he asserted that Congress has the power not only to protect rights against "unfriendly or insufficient state legislation," but also against state inaction, state "omission to pass laws for protection" (*id.* at 81). Since Congress cannot compel the acts of state officials, "the only appropriate legislation it can make is that which will operate directly on offenders and offenses," even though the administration of state laws might thereby be hindered (*id.* at 81–82; see also Frantz: 1362–63).

Similarly, in *United States v. Given* (25 F. Cas. 1324, C.C.D. Del. 1873, No. 15,210), Justice Strong observed that the Reconstruction amendments had enlarged the sphere of individual rights and had authorized Congress to enforce their guarantees against state officials and private persons as well.

> It was not intended to leave the right without full and adequate protection. Earlier prohibitions to the states were left without any express power of interference by Congress; but these later, encountering as they did so much popular prejudice and working changes so radical, were fortified by grants to Congress of power to carry them into full effect—that is, to enact any laws appropriate to give reality to the rights declared. (*Id.* at 1327)

Justice Strong further remarked, "[i]t is, I think, an exploded heresy that the national government cannot reach all individuals in the states" (*id.* at 1328). Thus, state action presented no problem; on the contrary, Strong perceived that private individuals are subject to federal enforcement jurisdiction when federal rights are violated. (See also Frantz: 1363–65.)

But these and other decisions supporting the intent underlying Reconstruction enforcement legislation were soon deeply compromised, ironically often with the participation of the same judges responsible for them. The Supreme Court's refusal to construe the work of the post-Civil War congresses in keeping with congressional intent coincided with the eating away of Reconstructionist will across the land—in fact was virtually the first pillar to go.

In *United States v. Reese* (92 U.S. 214, 1876), the Court invalidated a penal statute whose operation was not confined to the fifteenth amendment proscription against denial of the vote because of race, color, or previous condition of servitude (*id.* at 220–21). Unable to separate the constitutional from the unconstitutional portions of the legislation, "the Court simply held the questioned statute unconstitutional on its face because it extended federal power into some areas beyond those covered by the enabling provision of the amendment" (Tribe: 106–7).

The same day, the Court handed down its decision in *United States v. Cruikshank* (92 U.S. 542, 1876), the first Supreme Court test of fourteenth amendment enforcement legislation. The Court affirmed the earlier opinion of Justice Bradley, sitting in circuit. His opinion had invalidated a murder and conspiracy indictment against white defendants accused of mob massacre of a posse of blacks commissioned by a Republican sheriff in Louisiana (see *United States v. Cruikshank* 25 F. Cas. 707, C.C.D. La. 1874, No. 14,897). Bradley had reasoned in his circuit decision that the enforcement of fundamental rights guaranteed by the Constitution fell to the states. Congress had no authority "to perform the duty which the guaranty itself supposes it to be the duty of the state to perform" (*id.* at 710). But Bradley left open the door to federal enforcement if antecedent state failure to act could be shown.

The Supreme Court's affirmance of Justice Bradley's circuit court decision in *Cruikshank* dealt a fairly lethal blow to national enforcement powers under the thirteenth, fourteenth and fifteenth amendments. In practical effect, cases in which federal intervention could be invoked were narrowed to those featuring both clear racial motivation and clear state inaction. So the enforcement clauses of the new amendments and the intentions behind later implementing legislation were severely undercut.

Reese and *Cruikshank* notwithstanding, a number of cases decided by the Supreme Court in 1880 continued to leave open the possibility of national intervention to secure rights when states failed to do so. But the Court's decisions in *United States v. Harris* (1882) and the *Civil Rights Cases* (1883) are generally considered to have sealed the fate of federal enforcement powers against private individuals who act to violate the constitutional rights of other citizens. The nationalism of 1871 had faded, and the courts presided over a "progressive dismantling . . . of most of what Congress had attempted" (Frantz: 1373). Until the last two decades, the enforcement clauses of the Reconstruction era amendments were effectively eliminated as "vehicles for reaching private racial discrimination" (Estreicher: 452) and, *mutatis mutandis*, other sorts of discriminatory right-depriving conduct.

But evisceration of enforcement legislation was not mandated by *Harris* or by the *Civil Rights Cases*, for the orthodox reading of these decisions has been far too restrictive. Most commentators have concluded that the two decisions constituted a death knell for the national government's responsibility to ensure civil rights because they required overt state action before federal involvement might be triggered. But in reality, both cases simply reiterated Justice Bradley's circuit opinion in *United States v. Cruikshank*. His opinion had explicitly left open the possibility that when the state fails to act, Congress may intervene on the basis of the Reconstruction amendments and their enforcement clauses, the broadest of which is section 5 of the fourteenth amendment. If the states do not live up to their duties when violations of civil rights occur, then Congress may act, even directly to reach private individuals.

United States v. Harris offered an opinion by Justice Woods, earlier the author of the expansive circuit decision in *United States v. Hall*. Concerning the Ku Klux Klan Act, Woods said simply that if the presumption that the states will act to correct situations of right-deprivation is correct, then the amendment does not entitle Congress to act. "[W]hen . . . the laws of the State . . . recognize and protect the rights of all persons, the amendment imposes no duty and confers no power upon Congress" (106 U.S. at 639). This in brief was precisely Bradley's theory—state inaction must be shown in order to trigger federal redress. Only when the Klan Act is construed to refer directly to private persons "without reference to the laws of the State or their administration by her officers" (*id*. at 640) does it become an unwarranted broadening of the fourteenth amendment.

> Justice Woods is not adopting the extreme view that congressional enforcement power never extends to 'private acts.' He is adopting the view of Garfield and the moderates that it does not extend to such acts in the absence of some showing that state protection has failed or has been withheld. (Frantz: 1379)

The *Civil Rights Cases* took the same tack as *Harris*, despite the tendency of later generations to see in them the extreme view forbidding all federal government actions against private deprivations of rights. Justice Bradley's decision invalidated the portion of the Civil Rights Act of 1875 that was intended to give freedmen access to public accommodations. Bradley and the Court's eight-man majority declined to consider an innkeeper's refusal to serve blacks an incident or badge of slavery, and accordingly ruled that the enforcement powers of the thirteenth amendment could not reach such private discrimination (109 U.S. at 21). Nor, Bradley argued, did section 5 of the fourteenth amendment authorize federal intervention, since the wrongful act of an individual unsupported by state authority was "simply a private wrong" (*id*. at 17) and could not be redressed by congressional action. According to Bradley, the 1875 act was unconstitutional because it failed to lay the foundation for invoking the federal remedy:

> An inspection of the law shows that it makes no reference whatever to any supposed or apprehended violation of the Fourteenth Amendment on the part of the States. It is not predicated on any such view. It proceeds *ex directo* to declare that certain acts committed by individuals shall be deemed offences, and shall be prosecuted and punished by proceedings in the courts of the United States. It does not profess to be corrective of any constitutional wrong committed by the States; it does not make its operation to depend upon any such wrong committed. It applies equally to cases arising in States which have the justest laws respecting the personal rights of citizens, and whose authorities are ever ready to enforce such laws, as to those which arise in States that may have violated the prohibition of the amendment. In other words, it steps into the domain of local jurisprudence, and lays down rules for the conduct of individuals in society towards each other, and imposes sanctions for the enforcement of those rules, without referring in any manner to any supposed action of the State or its authorities. (*Id*. at 14)

If Justice Bradley had meant to forbid any possibility of federal redress for wrongful deprivation of civil rights, he would not have made this argument. His quarrel with the 1875 act was that it lumped all the states together and injected the federal government into local circumstances without an antecedent finding of state failure to carry out its duties under the fourteenth amendment. This is not to condemn any and all federal actions against private individuals alleged to have engaged in right-depriving discriminatory conduct. Rather, it reiterates Bradley's own circuit opinion in *United States v. Cruikshank*: state inaction must be shown before federal involvement may be triggered. Congressional enforcement power takes its "inception from the moment that the state fails to comply with the duty enjoined, or violates the prohibition imposed." Congress may not "perform the duty which the guaranty itself supposes it to be the duty of the state to perform, and which it requires the state to perform" (25 F. Cas. at 710). The states may not fail to provide for the equal treatment of citizens and, even in the face of the *Civil Rights Cases*, Congress may enforce provisions of the Reconstruction amendments when states fail to perform their obligations.

It is a misreading of these early cases to see in them a demand for positive state action before federal authority may step in to redress wrongs. All that is required is impotence or even custom such that states end up winking at wrongful deprivations of civil rights (see Frantz, *passim*). *Harris* and the *Civil Rights Cases*, while ambiguous, do not refute the kind of argument Judge Woods made in *United States v. Hall*: the states may not deny anyone equal protection of the laws.

> Denying includes inaction as well as action, and denying the equal protection of the laws includes the omission to protect, as well as the omission to pass laws for protection. (26 F. Cas. at 81)

The first Justice Harlan dissented in the *Civil Rights Cases*. Harlan took the position that the fourteenth amendment was self-enforcing because it granted state as well as federal citizenship to all native-born or naturalized persons (109 U.S. at 46). An affirmative congressional power to enforce the equal protection of the laws was therefore inherent in the amendment, making it unnecessary to wait for clear state failures to act (*id.* at 46–47). Harlan's dissent was not vindicated until Warren Court decisions in the 1960s (*e.g.*, *South Carolina v. Katzenbach*, 383 U.S. 301, 1966, and *Katzenbach v. Morgan*, 384 U.S. 641, 1966, discussed in Chapter 8). At the time his insistence that freedom from discrimination was a constitutional right directly enforceable by the national government drew little support.

> His views ran completely counter to the thinking of the contemporary white majority both in matters of political sovereignty and—though this was less frankly admitted—in matters of racial equality. (Pole: 343)

Justice Harlan relied on the idea that the Constitution now explicitly enjoined discrimination, and so the means to ensure protection must also be given directly to federal jurisdiction:

> [T]he Fourteenth Amendment's prohibition on state laws was an express limitation on the power of the state, but was never intended to diminish the nation's authority in protecting rights secured by the Constitution. (Pole: 192)

Harlan further maintained that the class tyranny of racial discrimination had been abolished by the Reconstruction amendments and that fundamental liberties enforceable by Congress had been established (109 U.S. at 52–56). If *de facto* discriminatory policies were to be permitted because of federal lack of oversight or because of judicial rulings acceding to a restrictive view of national authority, then the clear intentions giving rise to these new laws and their means of enforcement would be vitiated. And, prophetically, Harlan concluded that a course of inaction by the federal government would end up condoning discriminatory deprivation of rights not only of blacks but of other classes of victims as well (*id.* at 61–62).

For many decades after 1883, the *Civil Rights Cases* were interpreted by the courts to forbid federal legislative action framed to protect minority groups against private invidious discrimination. Not only was Justice Harlan's dissent ignored until recently, but also the nuances in Justice Bradley's reasoning for the majority were wholly disregarded. *United States v. Harris* and the *Civil Rights Cases* came to stand for the restrictive propositions that the fourteenth amendment speaks only to states and at the same time does not impose on states new affirmative duties to guarantee civil rights.

> It should be remembered that, while the chief present significance of the Civil Rights Cases lies in the analytical framework of Justice Bradley's opinion, with its suggestion that state tolerance of at least some private conduct might be state action, the decision in its own time, and for many subsequent years, was significant chiefly for its result: the invalidation of the Civil Rights Act of 1875 and the consequent denial to the federal government of any power to prevent the emergence of 'Jim Crow' *apartheid* in the South. This result was plainly wrong, not only morally and politically, but as a matter of constitutional law. (Tribe: 1153 n. 16)

That today we can see the wrong in this result is hardly mysterious, for now we are committed to eradicating *de facto* discrimination. The activist Warren Court handed the necessary power to Congress by reading the fourteenth amendment in the way Harlan did in 1883—states must act to protect rights and are prohibited from failing to act. When they do not, authority made available to the national government under statutes such as the Ku Klux Klan Act and the Enforcement Act may be exercised both in civil and criminal actions to secure in practice as well as in theory the fundamental egalitarian rights protected by the fourteenth amendment. And it may well be that the enforcement clause of the fourteenth amendment itself supplies requisite jurisdiction, as Harlan insisted in 1883 and as some modern courts have reiterated.

In the meantime, an "anomalous gap between obligation and enforcement" (Pole: 195) persisted, and the position of the federal courts, though wholly untenable, endured for generations. The fourteenth amendment prohibited the consequences of social prejudice, yet the courts continued to permit "the practices which were the normal and consistent expression of those prejudices" (Pole: 193). Because of judicial precedent and congressional lethargy, the existing domination of whites over blacks and discrimination against other minorities were allowed to stand until the latter half of the twentieth century. All three Reconstruction era amendments and the civil rights acts passed to enforce them received drastically restrictive interpretation for more than eighty years.

The fate of the Klan Act was typical. It languished virtually unused for decades only to meet a Supreme Court rendering in 1951 that utterly thwarted the goals of its framers. *Collins v. Hardyman* (341 U.S. 651, 1951) was a case brought under 42 U.S.C. section 1985(3). Plaintiffs, who were members of a political club, alleged a conspiracy to deny them equal privileges and immunities under the law after American Legionnaires broke up their peaceable meeting devoted to discussion of the Marshall Plan. The Court in effect held that that the suit should have been dismissed for failure to state a claim, since the Legionnaires were not acting under "color of law." Justice Jackson's majority opinion treated the skirmish as a simple assault case, finding no grounds for a federal civil rights claim. For section 1985(3) to come into play, conspirators must join for the express purpose of depriving persons or classes of persons of the equal protection of the laws or of equal privileges and immunities under the law. According to Justice Jackson:

> There is not the slightest allegation that defendants were conscious of or trying to influence the law, or were endeavoring to obstruct or interfere with it. The only inequality suggested is that the defendants broke up plaintiffs' meeting and did not break up meetings of others with whose sentiments they agreed. . . . Such private discrimination is not inequality before the law unless there is some manipulation of the law or its agencies to give sanction or sanctuary for doing so. Plaintiffs' rights were certainly invaded, disregarded and lawlessly violated. . . . [But their] rights *under the laws* and to *protection of the laws* remain untouched and equal to the rights of every other Californian, and may be vindicated in the same way and with the same effect as those of any other citizen who suffers violence at the hands of a mob. (*Id.* at 661–62, emphasis in original)

This restrictive construction of the Klan Act rendered it virtually useless as an avenue of redress for injured victims whose federal rights, in this case the right of peaceable assembly, were in fact compromised. On the Court's reading, section 1985(3) is no remedy at all, and that is the point struck by Justice Burton in dissent (joined by Justices Black and Douglas):

> Congress certainly has the power to create a federal cause of action in favor of persons injured by private individuals through the abridgement of federally created constitutional rights. It seems to me that Congress has done just this in [1985(3)]. (*Id.* at 664)

One reason that decisions such as *Collins* were routinely made in section 1985(3) cases was the deep fear that plaintiffs would jump state courts in a wide variety of circumstances that should be handled at the state level. To allow 1985(3) causes of action "'would open the door wide to every aggrieved litigant in a state court proceedings, and set the federal courts up as an arbiter of the correctness of every state decision'" (*Johnson v. Stone*, 268 F.2d 803, 805, 7th Cir. 1959, quoting from *Bottone v. Lindsley*, 170 F.2d 705, 707, 10th Cir. 1948, *cert. denied* 336 U.S. 944, 1949). Moreover, prior to the Warren Court, some courts distinguished carefully between federal rights and rights conferred by states and proceeded to hold that only the former are shielded by 1985(3). So, for example, rights such as security from assault, freedom from the prosecution's knowing use of perjured testimony, and privilege against false imprisonment were denied Klan Act coverage in cases during the last fifty years. And some courts quite erroneously even read into the language of 1985(3) a state action or state color of law requirement, which of course undercut the statute even further as a viable remedy. So the typical case before the Warren Court's corrective action warrants condemnation.

> The Supreme Court was horribly wrong in *Collins v. Hardyman* in ruling that the statute was not to be interpreted to reach private individuals who broke up a meeting of the plaintiffs. . . . This was a federally created right that was negated, within the constitutional competence of Congress and within the Congressional intent. The dissenting justices were correct. (Antieau: 136)

Private parties who conspire to deny federal constitutional rights are indeed liable under section 1985(3).

> [I]t is judicial legislation of the worst kind to superimpose a requirement that the plaintiff prove these conspirators 'manipulated,' 'influenced,' or 'interfered with' the law. (*Id.* at 137)

Griffin v. Breckenridge (403 U.S. 88, 1971) was the breakthrough case making possible accurate section 1985(3) judgments. A number of vital Warren Court cases during the 1960s prepared the way for the *Griffin* decision by revitalizing virtually all Reconstruction era legislation enforcing the thirteenth, fourteenth, and fifteenth amendments. *Griffin* brought the Klan Act into the trend. Some of these decisions have been characterized as "court-made law." Providing full equality under the law for blacks was indeed the Court's primary motivation. But as we have seen, these decisions were "soundly rooted in established constitutional principles" (Cox, 1966:107) and reflected the views of the post-Civil War Congresses that framed the early civil rights legislation.

An eighty-year failure of national will came to an end in the 1960s and the pursuit of equality, the engine of Republicans during Reconstruction, was put back on the track. Both Congress (Civil Rights Acts of 1964 and 1968) and the Supreme Court entered upon a renewed struggle to protect and preserve the rights of all American citizens. Constitutional protections owed members of despised minorities, including members of new religions, were enhanced and secured as a result. But there is still an ominous slip between theory and the decisions of some courts when cases similar to *Collins v. Hardyman* arise. So the practical implementation of legal guarantees of treatment of each person as an equal has by no means been fully consummated.

Chapter 8
The Impact of *Griffin v. Breckenridge*

> The Bradley-Harlan debate over congressional power to eliminate
> badges of slavery centered on the nature of the institution itself.
> The majority's failure in the *Civil Rights Cases* to recognize the
> realities of slavery and its legacy only postponed the inevitable
> acceptance of the position taken by Justice Harlan in dissent.
> Eighty-five years after the *Civil Rights Cases*, the Harlan posi-
> tion was vindicated by the Supreme Court in *Jones v. Alfred H.
> Mayer Co.* (Buchanan: 378)

Jones (392 U.S. 409, 1968) tested the authority of Congress under the
enforcement clause of the thirteenth amendment to reach private conduct that has the effect of perpetuating the badges and incidents of slavery. According to a portion of the Civil Rights Act of 1866 (now codified
at 42 U.S.C. section 1982), freedmen have the same right as whites to
hold and convey property. Claiming that the defendant refused to sell
him a house on the sole ground that he was black, Jones sued for injunctive and other relief for alleged private discriminatory deprivation of
rights. The Court could not have been more forceful in supporting Jones'
claim, and the idea that state action would be required for such a suit to
proceed should have been decisively put to rest.

> [W]hen racial discrimination herds men into ghettos and makes
> their ability to buy property turn on the color of their skin, then
> it too is a relic of slavery. (*Id.* at 442–43)

Congress, taking seriously its power to enforce the thirteenth amendment, had legislated in 1866 against such invidious discrimination in
property holding by private parties; in *Jones*, the Court declared the
exercise of that power constitutional. The *Jones* decision in effect overruled the *Civil Rights Cases* (Estreicher: 467). Ironically, the modern-
day Justice Harlan dissented, taking a position nearly opposite from that
of his earlier namesake on the necessity of state action question.

During its historic and groundbreaking 1965 term, the Supreme
Court handed down a number of decisions effectively erasing most
vestiges of the state color-of-law impediment to proper construction of
legislation enforcing the fourteenth and fifteenth amendments. There is
real innovation and novelty to be found in the Court's decisions.

> [They] emphasize the responsibility of Congress for human rights under the enforcement sections of the fourteenth and fifteenth amendments . . . and call attention to a vast untapped reservoir of federal legislative power to define and promote the constitutional rights of individuals in relation to state government. (Cox, 1966:99)

In *South Carolina v. Katzenbach* (383 U.S. 301, 1966), the Court struck down literacy tests in voting, sustaining the Voting Rights Act of 1965 as a proper exercise of congressional power under section 2 of the fifteenth amendment. The second sections of the thirteenth and fifteenth amendments are identical, providing that "[t]he Congress shall have power to enforce this article by appropriate legislation." Section 5 of the fourteenth amendment has the same substantive import: "The Congress shall have power to enforce, by appropriate legislation, the provisions of this article." If Congress has power to ensure individual voting rights under the enforcement section of the fifteenth amendment (*South Carolina v. Katzenbach*), and if it has power under the thirteenth to eliminate the relics of slavery (*Jones v. Alfred H. Mayer Co.*), nothing would seem to prevent proceeding in exactly the same way in fourteenth amendment matters, however more complex and however greater the threat of "overfederalization" that many people perceive.

A second 1965 term case, *Katzenbach v. Morgan* (384 U.S. 641, 1966), "not only illustrates the principle but indicates the Court's readiness to allow it the full sweep of its logical potential" (Cox, 1966:102). Once again, the constitutionality of the Voting Rights Act of 1965 was at issue. But the Court moved beyond the *South Carolina* circumstances and confirmed congressional authority to guarantee non-discriminatory treatment in voting and public services for the New York Puerto Rican community. Based on its reading of the enforcement section of the fourteenth amendment, the Court acted to protect equal treatment in advance of clear violations by the state. Section 5 for the first time was taken by the Court to include a broad grant of power analogous to that contained in the "necessary and proper clause" in article I, section 8 of the Constitution—power "authorizing Congress to exercise its discretion in determining whether and what legislation is needed to secure the guarantees of the Fourteenth Amendment" (384 U.S. at 650–51; see also Estreicher: 505–6). Congress can therefore act to prevent conduct that has not already been proven to violate fourteenth amendment guarantees.

> [T]he *Morgan* Court held that Congress may act in a broad prophylactic fashion to ensure that Puerto Ricans have the political power that will enable them 'better to obtain "perfect equality of civil rights and the equal protection of the laws."' (Estreicher: 506, quoting from 384 U.S. at 653)

And as Archibald Cox observes:

[T]he *Morgan* case left no doubt that section 5 of the fourteenth amendment gives Congress power to deal with conduct outside the scope of section 1 . . . where the measurement is a means of securing the state's performance of its fourteenth amendment duties, regardless of its past compliance or violations. (1966:103)

On the question whether section 5 also gives Congress the jurisdiction directly to reach private conduct, the bench of 1965–66 came close to taking an affirmative stand. Its disunity in the case of *United States v. Guest* (383 U.S. 745, 1966) is one reason that recent litigation under the Klan Act has produced contrary and confusing results in the lower courts—not least in cases brought by deprogrammed plaintiffs.

United States v. Guest tested the reach of the Enforcement Act of 1870 (now 18 U.S.C. section 241), the criminal analogue to the Klan Act. Section 241 makes it a federal offense to conspire to interfere with the free exercise of any right or privilege secured by the Constitution. In the *Guest* case, the defendants were a group of whites who murdered a black man driving through Georgia on his way to Washington, D.C. Justice Stewart's opinion for the Court perceived section 241 as remedial only, not extending to private conspiracies interfering with the exercise of rights under the equal protection clause in the absence of state action (*id.* at 754–55). By a circuitous route, Stewart was able to find state action and decided the case on those grounds (*id.* at 756–57).

But six justices in two different concurring opinions in *Guest* found congressional authority to reach private conspiratorial right-denying conduct in section 5 of the fourteenth amendment. Justice Clark declared in dictum that section 5 allows Congress "to enact laws punishing all conspiracies" that interfere with fourteenth amendment rights—with or without state action (*id.* at 762). Justice Brennan went even further in his concurring opinion. According to Brennan, any right secured by the Constitution is protected from private conspiratorial interference by section 241—in this case, the right to non-discriminatory access to state facilities arising under the fourteenth amendment (*id.* at 780). Thus, although the amendment itself speaks only in negative terms and only to the states, Justice Brennan read section 5 as authorizing Congress "to exercise its discretion in fashioning remedies to achieve civil and political equality for all citizens" (*id.* at 784).

The commitment of the national government to secure rights in practice was at stake in *United States v. Guest*. The struggle for racial equality was again on the move in the 1960s, and the Court was unwilling to leave the issue to politicians. Guest offered a majority view—Clark, Black, and Fortas in one concurrence, Brennan, Warren and Douglas in the other—that section 241 may reach private conspiratorial discriminatory wrongs. Underlying these opinions was the view that rights imply duties, and the cardinal duty is that one citizen may not deny another his free enjoyment of the rights granted to all citizens. It may be argued that isolated acts of violence must not bring federal power to bear, for pursuant to the division of labor between the federal government and the states, state courts adjudicate most criminal and civil actions. But under *Morgan* and *Guest*, the Supreme Court took cognizance of the fact that a pattern of wrongs may be indicated, and therefore utilization of federal authority may indeed be both legitimate and necessary.

> Congress may regulate individual instances which lack significance when taken in isolation, if cumulatively their regulation is appropriate to effectuating a constitutional objective. (Cox, 1966: 118)

Where racially based savagery takes place, state and local avenues of recourse may be unavailable, and that is exactly the reason that the Enforcement Act of 1870 and the Ku Klux Klan Act of 1871 were passed in the first place. The situation, I submit, is no different under circumstances of widespread persecution of fringe or minority religious groups. And on a liberal reading, the Court took that step in 1971 in the case of *Griffin v. Breckenridge* (403 U.S. 88).

Griffin saw a unanimous bench revive the conspiracy section of the Klan Act (now 42 U.S.C. section 1985[3]), remove from it any purported state action requirement, and make it accessible to minorities other than racial ones. As a result of the Court's decision, members of specifiable groups who find themselves subject to hostile acts by virtue of their group membership alone have potential redress in the form of a federal civil tort action allowing them to sue their tormentors for injunctive relief and compensatory and punitive damages.

Griffin effectively overruled *Collins v. Hardyman* on the state involvement question. White conspirators assaulted a group of blacks traveling in Mississippi, believing the blacks were organizing civil rights activities. No state officials were implicated: the case featured a purely private conspiracy of violent whites assaulting and beating peaceable blacks. Relying on *Collins*, the federal district court had dismissed plaintiffs' section 1985(3) action on the ground that there was no state action. The Fifth Circuit Court of Appeals affirmed the dismissal but expressed serious doubts about the disposition and clearly wished the Supreme Court to reexamine its reasoning in *Collins*. In doing so, the Court expressly disavowed its twenty-year-old decision:

> [I]t is clear, in the light of the evolution of decisional law in the years that have passed since that case was decided, that many of the constitutional problems there perceived simply do not exist. Little reason remains, therefore, not to accord to the words of the statute their apparent meaning. (*Id.* at 95–96)

And the words "fully encompass the conduct of private persons" (*id.* at 96). Nothing in the Klan Act's language about depriving other persons of the equal protection of the laws or equal privileges and immunities under the laws "requires the action working the deprivation to come from the State" (*id.* at 97).

> Indeed, the failure to mention any such requisite can be viewed as an important indication of congressional intent to speak in § 1985(3) of *all* deprivations of 'equal protection of the laws' and 'equal privileges and immunities under the laws,' whatever their source. (*Id.*, emphasis in original)

If the criminal enforcement statute (18 U.S.C. section 241) does not call for state involvement in order to trigger remedial action, then neither does its civil analogue require action by state officials before it may be brought into play. "To read any such requirement into § 1985(3) would thus deprive that section of all independent effect" (*id.* at 99)—that is, it would simply duplicate section 1983 (see Chapter 9). Writing for the Court, Justice Stewart quoted Representatives Shellabarger and Shanks, who played important roles in pushing the Klan Act through the Forty-second Congress. In Shanks's words:

> 'I do not want to see [this measure] so amended that there shall be taken out of it the frank assertion of the power of the national Government to protect life, liberty, and property, irrespective of the act of the State.' (Quoted in 403 U.S. at 101)

Justice Stewart continued that "all indicators—text, companion provisions, and legislative history—point unwaveringly to § 1985(3)'s coverage of private conspiracies" (*id.*). The restrictions on the usefulness of this federal remedy stem from the language requiring purposeful deprivation of equality. If equal protection and equal privileges and immunities are transgressed by a conspiracy directed at others, then some class-based or racial "invidiously discriminatory animus" (*id.* at 102) must lie behind the action of the conspirators. So in order to state a cause of action, plaintiffs in 1985(3) suits must allege: (1) a conspiracy, (2) whose purpose is deprivation of equal protection or equal privileges and immunities, (3) an act in furtherance of the conspiracy's object, whereby (4) another is injured in his person or property or deprived of exercising any right or privilege of a citizen (*id.* at 102–3).

At least three factors make *Griffin* a watershed decision, particularly for kidnapped and deprogrammed plaintiffs. First, the unanimous Court could not have been clearer in striking down a state action or state involvement requirement. Thus by extension, victims of forcible deprogramming may have a cause of action against their abductors even if a conservatorship order or police connivance or some other official action cannot be alleged. Second, the *Griffin* Court read section 1985(3) to include not only conspiracies based on race, but also conspiracies based on "otherwise class-based, invidiously discriminatory animus" (*id.* at 102). This reading opens 1985(3) suits to members of groups injured or discriminated against where the conspirators' motive is not racial hatred but rather, say, religious bigotry or some other kind of animus. The Court did not define what counts as a class for 1985(3) purposes, leaving lower courts to their own devices and thereby creating persistent disagreement. Third, *Griffin* found congressional sources of authority favoring the black plaintiffs in the enforcement clause of the thirteenth amendment and in alleged deprivation of their constitutionally protected right to interstate travel (*id.* at 105–6). But the Court explicitly left open the question whether some other source of congressional jurisdiction could have been brought to the fore as well, and specifically referred to the enforcement clause of the fourteenth amendment.

> In identifying these two constitutional sources of congressional power, we do not imply the absence of any other. More specifically, the allegations of the complaint in this case have not required consideration of the scope of the power of Congress under § 5 of the Fourteenth Amendment. (*Id.* at 107)

This aspect of *Griffin* is crucial, for where the facts do not permit deprogrammed plaintiffs to allege deprivation of the right to travel, they may be obliged to rely on the fourteenth amendment's enforcement clause as a source of congressional authority. The lower courts have been deeply divided on this issue during the last decade, as the following cases illustrate.

In *Dombrowski v. Dowling* (459 F.2d 190, 1972), the Seventh Circuit Court of Appeals dismissed a section 1985(3) suit by a lawyer who was refused office space by a real estate management firm because of the character of his largely minority-group clientele. The court predicated its ruling on the lack of state involvement in the alleged discrimination (*id.* at 196). But a 1985(3) action was upheld by the Fifth Circuit Court of Appeals in *Westberry v. Gilman Paper Co.* (507 F.2d 206, 1975). An environmental activist brought suit against his employers and their agents, claiming that they were attempting to harm, even kill him. While wholly private, the court nonetheless concluded that the cause of action fell under the terms of 1985(3) (*id.* at 210).

Among the more interesting of the section 1985(3) suits that have found favor in the courts is *Action v. Gannon* (450 F.2d 1227, 8th Cir. 1971). The Eighth Circuit Court of Appeals took the step left open by the *Griffin* Court and found a congressional source of authority for punishing private conspiracies in section 5 of the fourteenth amendment. The plaintiffs in *Action v. Gannon* were members of a predominately white Roman Catholic parish seeking injunctive relief against disruption of their services by two black human rights groups (Action and the Black

Liberation Front). The appeals court held that the parishioner-plaintiffs could avail themselves of a section 1985(3) cause of action, that section 5 of the fourteenth amendment provided a constitutional source of power to reach the right-denying conspiracy, and that injunctive relief was available so long as the first amendment rights of the defendants were not abridged in the process. The circuit court followed *Griffin* step-by-step with the exception of the source-of-authority issue. On that question, the court consciously accepted what it regarded as an invitation by the *Griffin* Court to rely upon the fourteenth amendment's enforcement clause to authorize section 1985(3) suits where neither the thirteenth amendment nor the right to travel interstate might be invoked. "We think it . . . clear that Congress had power to reach this conspiracy under §§ 1 and 5 of the Fourteenth Amendment" (*id.* at 1233). Reasoning that the fourteenth amendment incorporated the first amendment's right to free assembly and worship, the circuit court in *Action v. Gannon* went on to utilize section 5 as a proper source of authority, pursuant to implied *Griffin* requirements for establishing federal jurisdiction and the availability of a federal remedy in subsequent 1985(3) cases. The opinion referred to *United States v. Guest* at this point:

> In *Guest*, six Justices—Warren, Black, Douglas, Clark, Brennan, and Fortas—expressed the view that Congress has power under § 5 of the Fourteenth Amendment to punish private conspiracies that interfere with Fourteenth Amendment rights. (*Id.* at 1235)

The court continued:

> While the Court in *Griffin* left the door open for a reexamination of *Guest*, we do not believe that it will reject the majority views expressed therein. The Fourteenth Amendment and § 1985(3), construed in *Griffin*, are too closely related with respect to date of passage, authorship, and purpose to permit such a result with consistency. (*Id.* at 1236)

Action v. Gannon also supports the view that the legislative history of the Klan Act undergirded the power of the federal government to punish private right-denying conspiracies.

The commentators, as well as the courts, are still deeply divided over these issues. Avins, for example, would permit virtually none of the steps taken by the *Action* court (see 43 Notre Dame Law. 317, 1968, and 11 St. Louis U.L.J. 331, 1967). His position is endorsed by the authors of several other law review articles (*e.g.*, Fockele, 46 U. Chi. L. Rev. 402, 1979, and Kreidman, 52 B.U.L. Rev. 599, 1972). Two other analyses support the plausibility of section 1985 suits (Note, 74 Yale L.J. 1462, 1965, and Wildman, 17 San Diego L. Rev. 317, 1980). Two more explicitly endorse the approach taken by the Eighth Circuit Court of Appeals in *Action v. Gannon* (see Malpass, 54 N.C.L. Rev. 677, 1976, and Calkins, 37 Mo. L. Rev. 525, 1972). Still others fall between the extremes (Note, 45 Geo. Wash. L. Rev. 239, 1977, and Brophy, 1973 Law & Soc. Order 639).

Critics of *Action*, and sometimes even *Griffin*, contend that if such 1985(3) suits are allowed, then we face a radical and impermissible shifting of the balance between federal and state authorities, potentially eroding the foundations of a republican form of government. Technically, lawyers call this fear the federalization of tort law. In my view, *Griffin* built in sufficient limitations on the sorts of circumstances under which a section 1985(3) action can be maintained: there must be a conspiracy based on racial or other kind of class hatred and there must be some constitutional source of power. Even if there were agreement on this understanding of the meaning of *Griffin*, however, there would still be arguments over the source of power issue. The deprogramming cases offer good illustrations of the different routes courts are taking in deciding that matter. And finally, disagreement continues over what constitutes a class for section 1985(3) purposes.

Plaintiffs must establish that they are members of a clearly definable group and that their victimization occurred by virtue of membership. The Fifth Circuit Court of Appeals used a loose "intellectual nexus" standard in *Westberry v. Gilman Paper Co.*: the class "must have an intellectual nexus which has somehow been communicated to, among and by the members of the group" (507 F.2d at 215). Other courts have required a stricter criterion, namely that the group be well-established and easily recognizable—vague political and ideological ties are not sufficient. Nor is a class constituted by the conduct of the defendants. Sharing the trait of victim as a result of actions taken by defendants will not forge a class for section 1985(3) purposes. The most severe limiting yardstick that courts have used is that members of a qualifying class possess "'discrete, insular, and immutable'" characteristics comparable to race, national origin, or sex (Note, 64 Minn. L. Rev. at 650). These are traits for which the individual bears no responsibility, but the critera are overly restrictive and are also at odds with congressional intent at the time of passage of the Klan Act. Middle ground has been occupied by courts defining a protected class as one that has been discriminated against in the past and that constitutes a minority akin to a racial minority. Some courts considering deprogramming cases have used this criterion to cover new or marginal religious movements. This definition is broad enough to protect "suspect-like" classes, for example, aliens, ex-convicts, and the handicapped, while excluding groups that, say, merely share a political ideology (*id.* at 651–52).

One way to include unpopular political or ideological groups as classes for section 1985(3) purposes without permitting immediate filing of any and all tort cases at the federal level is to restrict the circumstances under which the remedy may be invoked. On this approach the plaintiff would have the burden of showing that he was engaged in the exercise of his fundamental rights at the time a conspiracy against him was carried out. This is a conceivable rationale for cases such as *Action v. Gannon*: white Roman Catholic parishioners may not qualify as a "suspect-like" group, but their rights to free assembly and free religious exercise were threatened by the conspiracy of black militants. So they both shared a close intellectual or ideological tie defining them as a group and were engaged in carrying out a basic constitutional right. Something like this approach both narrows the kinds of groups that qualify under section 1985(3) and at the same time avoids a vague and difficult-to-apply standard such as merely sharing an intellectual nexus. Interestingly, professional deprogrammers recently brought a 1985(3) suit and failed to qualify themselves as a sufficiently identifiable and discriminated-against class (*Alexander v. Unification Church of America*, 634 F.2d 673, 678, 2d Cir. 1980).

Following *Griffin*, a final burden falling upon section 1985(3) plaintiffs is to show that defendants' motives are indeed invidiously discriminatory, and that the conspiracy is propelled by that animus. Some courts have required plaintiffs to prove that persons not in their class or group would have been treated differently by the conspirators, or that the conspiracy would not have been formed in the first place except by virtue of the victim's group membership. In other words, mere personal animus is not sufficient. But since the motive of the conspirators is at issue, this burden on the plaintiff should be limited. At some point, the burden must shift to the defendants to show that class-based animus is not the ruling factor in the actions alleged to have been taken by them against the plaintiff.

> Although an animus in others alone is not sufficient, a plaintiff should be given the opportunity to demonstrate a connection or concerted action that links the defendant to those possessing the animus. Similarly, personal animus alone should not be sufficient to allow recovery under section 1985[3]; but courts should find that the animus requirement has been satisfied whenever a class-based motive is established, despite the presence of additional motives. In addition, courts should dismiss an action at the pleadings stage only when it appears certain that the plaintiffs are entitled to no relief under any interpretation of the facts that could be proved to support their claims. (Note, 64 Minn. L. Rev. at 665)

According to this approach, no quick dismissals or summary judgments in favor of the defendants would be handed down by the courts in the absence of a thorough examination of the defendants' motives; moreover, the burden would be on the defendants to show that their actions were not taken because of racial hatred or religious bigotry, for example. The deprogramming cases are complicated because they usually involve hired agents of beleaguered parents, and the motivations of the deprogrammers in a kidnapping action are obviously fiduciary as well as inspired by persecutory zeal. But the conspiracy comes into existence by virtue of a person's membership in a group, and that is not difficult for deprogrammed plaintiffs to show.

Following and extending *Griffin v. Breckenridge*, maintenance of a section 1985(3) cause of action requires proof that the class or group in question is protected for reasons such as past discrimination, that it has close and identifiable intellectual (or ritualistic) ties, or that fundamental rights are threatened by a conspiracy formed by virtue of the member's group alliance. Plaintiffs further must show that they actually are members of the protected group, or, sometimes, sufficiently associated with it to count. And finally, plaintiffs must demonstrate that the defendants' conspiratorial conduct is motivated by the plaintiffs' group membership or that the conspiracy would not have arisen in the absence of such group ties. Most courts hearing cases of kidnapped and deprogrammed plaintiffs have examined these elements to determine the availability of section 1985(3) coverage and have permitted the causes of action to go forward. Along with *Griffin v. Breckenridge*, the deprogramming cases have become further building blocks in the foundations of individual constitutional rights and religious liberties.

PART III

The Law Governing
Forcible Deprogramming

Chapter 9
Deprogramming Cases Under Section 1985(3)

The Forty-second Congress built discrete causes of action into sections 1 and 2 of the Civil Rights Act of 1871. Both causes of action were designed to buttress racial equality in practice. Section 1 of the act incorporated a state action requirement; under what is now 42 U.S.C. section 1983, persons acting under color of law to deprive others of constitutional rights may be sued for damages in federal court by the victim.

> Every person who, under color of any statute, ordinance, regulation, custom, or usage, of any State or Territory, subjects, or causes to be subjected, any citizen of the United States or other person within the jurisdiction thereof to the deprivation of any rights, privileges, or immunities secured by the Constitution and laws, shall be liable to the party injured in an action at law, suit in equity, or other proper proceeding for redress.

Section 2 of the Klan Act did not contain a state action requirement; that is to say that what is now 42 U.S.C. section 1985(3) did not simply duplicate section 1983. The distinction is crucial for nearly all cases involving deprogrammed plaintiffs, as the decisions discussed below demonstrate. The text of section 1985(3) is set forth in Chapter 6.

In *Griffin v. Breckenridge*, as we have seen, the Supreme Court specified the circumstances in which section 1985(3) might be invoked. The Court expressly disavowed any state action requirement, as its framers plainly intended. Thus the section reaches purely private right-denying conspiracies. Rights either to interstate travel or to protection against involuntary servitude were sanctioned as sources of congressional authority to reach private conspiracies that victimize members of minority groups. But the Court left the door open to other possible derivations of authority, including section 5 of the fourteenth amendment. This view is supported by the Court's decisions in *Katzenbach v. Morgan* and *United States v. Guest*, discussed in Chapter 8. And implicitly, other sources of authority such as the commerce clause and the first amendment may be available. The right to religious free exercise is fully protected so long as no vital state interest is compromised by a religious practice or by a religious prohibition of acts mandated by government.

Numerous cases involving abducted and forcibly restrained members of minority religious groups have appeared on court dockets during the last decade. Three have proceeded through the federal court system to the United States Supreme Court, which has denied certiorari in each instance. The cases are *Rankin v. Howard* (457 F. Supp. 70, D. Ariz. 1978, *rev'd*, 633 F.2d 844, 9th Cir. 1980, *cert. denied*, 451 U.S. 939, 1982); *Ward v. Connor* (495 F. Supp. 434, E.D. Va. 1980, *rev'd*, 657 F.2d 45, 4th Cir. 1981, *cert. denied*, 455 U.S. 907, 1982); and *Taylor v. Gilmartin* (434 F. Supp. 909, W.D. Okla. 1977, *rev'd*, 686 F.2d 1346, 10th Cir. 1982, *cert. denied*, 103 S.Ct. 788, 1983). Denial of certiorari simply means that the Supreme Court declines to hear a case for any of a number of undisclosed reasons, thereby permitting the immediately preceding decision to stand.

One would at first sight think that the circumstances surrounding deprogramming cases—adult citizens snatched off street corners, victims handcuffed to bedposts in motel rooms, all-night marathon shouting matches, covert smuggling of the exhausted and thoroughly frightened body to different locations—are so bizarre, and the illegalities of it all so blatant, that no case law of any importance could possibly arise from them. Just the opposite is true. While the lawlessness of kidnapping and forcible restraint may be apparent, district attorneys and prosecutors throughout the 1970s were extraordinarily reluctant to bring criminal charges against kidnappers hired by parents and especially against parents or relatives themselves. And in cases where charges were brought, a good faith defense or defense of justification more often than not seduced judges and juries into acquittals (see, *e.g.*, *United States v. Patrick*, 532 F.2d 142, 9th Cir. 1976). As a consequence, deprogramming victims were forced into federal courts to seek civil redress from their tormentors, availing themselves of the remedy *Griffin* provided minority groups whose members are persecuted for other than racial reasons. And, the grotesque and novel nature of the cases notwithstanding, "[t]he cult deprogramming damages cases may well resolve the single most compelling question left unanswered in *Griffin v. Breckenridge*" (Vermeire: 111). That question is the source of congressional power to reach a private conspiracy. Under *Griffin*, no court hearing a deprogrammed plaintiff's case brought under section 1985(3) can avoid making a decision on the source of power issue. Thus decisions in the deprogramming cases are significant because innovations may be forged in broad areas of constitutional law, not simply in law about religious liberties.

Rankin v. Howard was filed in federal district court in Arizona. Plaintiff Marcus Rankin was an adult member of the Unification Church whose father obtained a temporary guardianship over his son after arranging an *ex parte* or non-adversarial hearing before a Kansas judge. The father's application falsely alleged that his son was a resident of the Kansas county where the judge had jurisdiction. Rankin was brought to Kansas, taken into custody on the strength of the *ex parte* order and then flown to Phoenix, where deprogramming was unsuccessfully attempted under the auspices of the Freedom of Thought Foundation (457 F. Supp. at 71–72). He subsequently sued the lawyers for the Foundation, the Kansas judge, his parents and the deprogrammers, alleging a conspiracy to deprive him of his civil rights and various common law torts.

The defending judge and lawyers moved for summary judgment on the civil rights causes of action brought by Rankin under sections 1983 and 1985(3). A summary judgment proceeding provides a means of determining whether the issues raised in a case are substantial enough to warrant a trial; a motion for summary judgment will be granted only when there are no genuine issues of material fact and the moving party is entitled to judgment as a matter of law. The federal district court ruled that the Kansas judge who had granted the guardianship order was clothed by judicial immunity and accordingly granted his motion for summary judgment. Because available precedent seemed to indicate that only the judge could provide the state action needed for maintenance of the section 1983 cause of action, the other defendants were awarded derivative summary judgment on the 1983 cause on the ground that they could not have been acting under color of state law (*id.* at 73–74).

But the Arizona district court ruled that Rankin had succeeded in stating a cause of action under section 1985(3)—that he had established the elements set forth in *Griffin v. Breckenridge*. In particular, the court found that Rankin satisfied the mandate that a conspiracy be rooted in a class-based, invidiously discriminatory animus. The court accepted his allegation that Unification Church members constituted a class for purposes of section 1985(3), declaring that it had been unable to find any cases in which courts had refused to accept jurisdiction under 1985(3) when the asserted class was a religious one (*id.* at 74). The court was also satisfied with Rankin's allegation that the conspirators had been motivated by their abhorrence of the Unification Church. Moreover, the district court ruled that Rankin had succeeded in identifying a source of congressional power to reach the private conspiracy he had alleged, in that he had clearly been deprived of his constitutional right to interstate travel (*id.* at 75).

Marcus Rankin appealed what was already a substantial victory. The Ninth Circuit Court of Appeals handed him a further triumph by ruling that the Kansas judge might not in fact be immune if he knowingly participated in a conspiracy to violate Rankin's rights.

> If, as alleged, Judge Zeller knew the jurisdictional allegations to be fraudulent, or if valid Kansas statutes expressly foreclosed personal jurisdiction over a proposed ward in *ex parte* proceedings for temporary guardianship, then the judge acted in the clear and complete absence of personal jurisdiction. If his acts were part of a conspiracy, he is properly held responsible for the consequences. (633 F.2d at 849)

The appellate court also reversed the district court's holding that the judge's immunity derivatively protected the defendant deprogrammers. Thus if private persons corruptly conspire with a judge, they act under color of state law and may be held liable in a section 1983 action. As a consequence of the ninth circuit decision and the later denial of certiorari by the Supreme Court, Rankin's section 1983 cause of action could proceed in the district court along with his previously recognized section 1985(3) action.

In *Ward v. Connor*, a Virginia federal district court dismissed the section 1985(3) suit of a deprogrammed Unification Church plaintiff against his abductors. Reading 1985(3) narrowly, the district judge concluded that members of the Unification Church did not qualify as a class, that the defendants' benevolent concern negated the requisite discriminatory animus, and that alleged deprivation of the right to travel was secondary to claimed interference with Ward's first amendment rights of freedom of religion and association. The court accordingly held that the test set forth in *Griffin v. Breckenridge* had not been satisfied (495 F.Supp. at 437–38).

The Fourth Circuit Court of Appeals reversed the Virginia district court on all points, finding that the Unification Church was a class for section 1985 purposes, that the required discriminatory motive existed, and that alleged deprivation of the right to travel was sufficient to withstand the defendants' motion to dismiss (657 F.2d at 48). Since the congressional source of authority question was resolved by claimed deprivation of travel rights, the court of appeals declined to consider whether section 5 of the fourteenth amendment conferred power to reach the conspiracy (*id.* n. 5). Thus, even though the right to travel was only incidental to Ward's loss of his first amendment right to free religious exercise, it was sufficient to invoke one source of congressional authority specifically endorsed by the Supreme Court in *Griffin v. Breckenridge*.

The decisions in *Rankin* and *Ward* were significant victories for deprogrammed plaintiffs seeking redress in the courts for what they have experienced as profoundly insulting injuries to their rights to equality—in short, to their dignity as citizens and their rights to define their own beliefs. *Rankin* is the more important of the two cases because the appellate court permitted maintenance of causes of action under both sections 1983 and 1985(3). But neither case addressed the question whether section 5 of the fourteenth amendment is available as a source of power to reach private right-denying conspiracies.

The decision of the Tenth Circuit Court of Appeals in *Taylor v. Gilmartin* finally answered the fourteenth amendment source of authority question in the affirmative. The answer is qualified: it does not sweep away a state action requirement. Nonetheless, the decision seems destined to have significant practical and substantive ramifications for certain deprogrammed plaintiffs who are unable to demonstrate that their abductors have interfered with their right to travel.

Walter Taylor was a resident of the monastery of the Holy Protection of the Blessed Virgin Mary in Oklahoma City, Oklahoma. His parents, who were opposed to his religious affiliation, employed the Freedom of Thought Foundation to deprogram their adult son. As part of the scheme, Taylor's father applied to an Oklahoma state court to be appointed his son's temporary guardian. The judge granted the application, concluding that the parents' right to know that their son had decided to spend the rest of his life secluded in a monastery overrode "'any individual right [Plaintiff] might possibly have on a temporary basis . . . to be free from . . . custody'" (686 F.2d at 1349, quoting from the record in the guardianship proceeding). Taylor was taken from Oklahoma to Ohio and subjected to deprogramming under the temporary guardianship order. He was subsequently moved to Phoenix, Arizona, for the rehabilitation phase of the deprogramming. He escaped, returned to the seminary in Oklahoma City, and filed an action in Oklahoma federal district court against his parents and their hired deprogrammers. He alleged civil rights claims under sections 1983 and 1985(2) and (3) and various common law causes of action, including false imprisonment (id. at 1348–50). Section 1985(2) provides a federal cause of action to a person injured by a conspiracy to obstruct justice with intent to deny equal protection of the laws.

The district court dismissed the section 1983 action, rejecting Taylor's contention that the deployment of the Oklahoma judge and local police in the guardianship proceeding was tantamount to state action. The court also granted partial summary judgment on the 1985(2) and (3) causes on the ground that Congress did not have power to reach a private conspiracy to violate rights protected under the fourteenth amendment. Finally, the district court judge granted a directed verdict to the defendants on the false imprisonment charge, based on his conclusion that the temporary guardianship order was proper.

On appeal, the tenth circuit affirmed the district court's dismissal of the section 1983 cause of action, finding that 1983's color of law requirement had not been met under the facts of the case. The appellate court observed that the judge from whom the temporary guardianship order had been obtained had allowed himself to be used but was not a part of the conspiracy (id. at 1355). But the court of appeals reversed the district court on two crucial points. First, the court invalidated the temporary guardianship order on the grounds that the judge had acted in the complete absence of statutory jurisdiction and further that he had failed to provide proper notice of the guardianship hearing (id. at 1352–53). Second, the court held that Taylor might seek redress under sections 1985(2) and (3) even though it found that the factual circumstances did not lend themselves to a claim of interference with the right to interstate travel (id. at 1358).

As required by *Griffin v. Breckenridge*, the tenth circuit initially satisfied itself that the elements of a section 1985(3) action were present. In considering whether there had been class-based invidious discrimination, the court declared:

> It should be emphasized that these defendants are professionals. They perform this service for money and they spend a significant amount of time on it. The record shows that and certainly their conduct is odious and has the effect of depriving the victim of important rights—his liberty, his freedom, his right to practice his religion, among other rights. (*Id.* at 1357)

Because it did not give credence to Taylor's claim that he had been deprived of his right to travel, the court looked instead to the fourteenth amendment as the source of power to reach the conspiracy alleged. The court recognized that traditionally, the fourteenth amendment has provided no protection against private action (*id.* at 1358). But the court found sufficient state involvement in the cooperation of the judge and police officers to open a source of authority in section 5 of the amendment.

> In the case at bar, . . . the allegations extend beyond the private deprivation of constitutional rights. The contention is that the defendants formed a conspiracy *to cause the state to participate and deprive the plaintiff* of his liberty without due process and to interfere with his first amendment freedom of association and religion due to their hatred of minority religions. (*Id.* at 1358, emphasis in original)

The court examined the opinions subscribed to by the concurring justices in *United States v. Guest*, and declared itself in accord with the position taken there (*id.*):

> [A] private conspiracy which interferes with fourteenth amendment rights by preventing the state from granting equal treatment or by causing the state to deprive a citizen of his constitutional rights is sufficient state action within the power of Congress to remedy under § 5 of the fourteenth amendment, notwithstanding the state is not actually one of the conspirators. (*Id.* at 1359–60)

The appellate court also found Justice Stewart's majority view in *Guest* compatible with its own. However unwitting, the activity of the state judge and police officers "brought the state into a position which was tainted" (*id.* at 1360). The court accordingly held that "a private conspiracy . . . motivated by a class-based, invidiously discriminatory animus, to induce the state to violate one's first and fourteenth amendment rights is remedied by § 1985(2) and (3)" (*id.*).

The tenth circuit court concluded its opinion by condemning recourse to guardianship or conservatorship statutes to obtain court protection for deprogramming, when the proposed ward is an adult who does not show any evidence of insanity (*id.* at 1361). Referring to the opinion in *Katz v. Superior Court*, discussed in Chapter 2, the court observed that Taylor's exposure to the monastery had not had any gravely disabling adverse effects upon him. Taylor was not a "helpless child," but rather a person whose resolve was demonstrated by the fact that he had escaped and was still living at the monastery at the time of trial. According to the court:

> [T]his is a situation in which there is a gross concerted interference with a very fundamental right, the right to choose one's religion, and it is this underlying factor that makes the case actionable, or which greatly aggravates it. (*Id.* at 1362)

As noted earlier, the Supreme Court denied certiorari, thereby permitting the tenth circuit decision to stand.

The circuit decision in *Taylor v. Gilmartin* follows the lead of Justice Stewart's opinion for the Court in *Guest* in finding sufficient state involvement to permit invocation of section 5 of the fourteenth amendment as a source of power to reach a private conspiracy. It thus begs the question whether section 5 reaches private conspiracies in the absence of conduct on the part of conspirators to induce the state to deprive a citizen of constitutional rights.

Nonetheless, the decision is significant. Even when a member of a persecuted religious group cannot prove interference with the right to travel, *Taylor* permits maintenance of a section 1985(3) cause of action against private persons who conspire to enlist the state to act as an unwitting accomplice in their scheme to deprive the member of his first and fourteenth amendment rights. Arguably, the focus is on the conspiracy to induce state participation, not on the character or extent of any official participation thay may ensue. As a practical consequence, conspirators can be sued in federal court for attempting deprogramming under a conservatorship or guardianship order obtained for that purpose. Implicitly, the conspirators could defeat the cause of action by proving both that the conservatorship or guardianship proceeding satisfied due process requirements and that the proposed conservatee or ward was in fact a proper object of *parens patriae* solicitude under the governing statute. It remains to be seen what other sorts of private inducements to the state to violate the first and fourteenth amendments will be sufficient to support maintenance of section 1985(3) causes of action. But no matter how subsequent case law fleshes out *Taylor*, the decision makes federal recourse potentially available to new religious movement members who have been deprogrammed pursuant to conservatorship or guardianship orders.

All of the deprogramming cases are heavily tinged by high emotion on both sides, and of course both sides feel deeply that fundamental rights are at stake. Parents are genuinely distraught by the religious choices that their offspring have made, but most courts have held that parental anguish cannot excuse gross lawlessness. Tactical questions also abound: for example, plaintiffs' attorneys are loath to attempt recovery of damages in large amounts from parents because of unsympathetic juries, so they often ask only for token compensatory damages from parents and high compensatory and punitive damages from hired deprogrammers abetting the conspiracy. Punitive damages set an example, and the more deprogrammers are successfully sued, the more difficult and unpromising the profession in its 1970s vigilante justice form will become.

Other recent lower court cases offer factual circumstances similar to *Rankin*, *Ward*, and *Taylor*, and I shall refer to a few of them in order to establish the pattern. In *Cooper v. Molko* (512 F.Supp. 563, N. D. Cal. 1981), a federal district court declined to dismiss a Unification Church member's sections 1983 and 1985(3) causes of action against his parents, deprogrammers and police officers. In finding that the plaintiff had sufficiently alleged interference with rights protected under section 1985(3), the court declared explicitly that the loving motivation of the parents was not sufficient to negate claimed discriminatory animus against his religious group (*id.* at 569–70). Following *Griffin v. Breckenridge*, the court found the requisite source of authority to reach the conspiracy in the defendants' interference with the plaintiff's right to travel (*id.* at 570–71).

In *Bavis v. McKenna* (No. H-77-793, slip op., D. Md. Jan. 19, 1979), various defendants including a state court judge and deprogrammers moved to dismiss causes of action brought under sections 1983 and 1985(3). The plaintiff, a member of the International Society for Krishna Consciousness, had been deprogrammed in various places under color of an *ex parte* guardianship order obtained by her mother. The federal district judge dismissed the guardianship-granting judge on the ground that he was judicially immune from suit, but allowed the causes of action to stand against the remaining defendants. The court refused good faith as a defense at that stage of the proceeding: for benign motivation to qualify as a defense, defendants must show that they believed their actions to be lawful and that their belief was reasonable under the circumstances. The court further concluded that discrimination based on religious affiliation is actionable under section 1985(3), and that even if a conspiracy is wholly private in character, a 1985(3) action can be maintained if the object of the conspiracy is to deprive a plaintiff of the right to interstate travel or to "'cause state action which interferes with protected activities . . .'" (*id.* at 12).

Similarly, in *Augenti v. Cappellini* (84 F.R.D. 73, M.D. Pa. 1979), the court held that a Unification Church member's section 1985(3) claim was sufficient to withstand the defendants' motion for summary judgment. The judge ruled that the plaintiff's allegations satisfied *Griffin v. Breckenridge*, deferring until trial the defendants' claim that they lacked the requisite invidiously discriminatory animus because their motivation was benign (*id*. at 78).

While these cases seem to follow a typical pattern, their casts of characters and circumstances vary. Sometimes members of established, not novel, religious groups have been involved. Deprogramming has also been attempted on a lesbian because of her sexual preference; she brought a subsequent section 1985(3) suit. In another 1985 case, Reverend Moon was subpoenaed from an upstairs courtroom where his tax case was being tried and was subjected to many hours of virtually inquisitional questioning, clearly in violation of *Ballard* and *Cantwell*. The proceedings were subsequently quashed by intervention of a higher court. And in one notorious section 1985 action, a two million dollar damage suit was brought by a plaintiff who had been kidnapped and subjected to deprogramming intended to persuade her to abandon her long-standing membership in The Divine Light Mission. She happened to be a physician at New York Hospital, a Yale-educated graduate of Cornell Medical School held incommunicado for fifteen days until she faked a recantation. Obviously, the principles are the same in cases involving younger and more bootless members of society, but her case provides a particularly jarring illustration of illegal abduction and forcible deprogramming.

Several cases with results contrary to those discussed previously in this chapter appear in the literature and are championed by those seeking to extricate new religious group members from their affiliations. In *Weiss v. Patrick* (453 F.Supp. 717, D.R.I., *aff'd*, 588 F.2d 818, 1st Cir. 1978, *cert. denied*, 442 U.S. 929, 1979), the federal district court granted the defendants' motion to dismiss a section 1985(3) action and pendant state claims. Plaintiff was a member of the Unification Church; on the pretext of a Thanksgiving dinner with friends, her terminally ill mother arranged for her to meet deprogrammer Ted Patrick. The court discounted the plaintiff's testimony that she had been coerced and intimidated into feigning acquiescence with the deprogramming efforts. The judge found that the defendants' actions constituted "a proper exercise of their constitutional right to speak freely to a willing listener" (453 F.Supp. at 722). The judge further held that the plaintiff had failed to prove injury or the existence of a class-based animus, as required by *Griffin v. Breckenridge*. According to the court, the plaintiff's mother was motivated not by abhorrence of the Unification Church but rather by maternal solicitude for a daughter's health and well-being (*id*. at 724). The remaining defendants, as agents for the mother, were said to have derived their motivation from her solicitude.

The Minnesota Supreme Court took a similar tack in *Peterson v. Sorlien* (299 N.W.2d 123, 1980). Plaintiff, a member of The Way International, had sued her parents and deprogrammers in state court for false imprisonment and intentional infliction of emotional distress. The jury exonerated all the defendants on the false imprisonment charge but awarded nominal and punitive damages on the intentional infliction of emotional distress charge against the two defendants principally responsible for the deprogramming effort. Plaintiff Peterson appealed, and the Minnesota court affirmed the jury verdict.

Dealing first with the false imprisonment charge, the court uncritically and with but two references noted the emergence of "youth-oriented or pseudo-religious groups which utilize the techniques of what has been termed 'coercive persuasion' or 'mind control'. . ." (*id*. at 126). One reference was to Professor Delgado's law review article, "Religious Totalism: Gentle and Ungentle Persuasion under the First Amendment" (51 S. Cal. L. Rev. 1, 1977); the second was to Webster's definition of the word "cult" (299 N.W.2d at 126). A majority of the court found that plaintiff Peterson had resisted the deprogrammers during the first three days of her captivity but had willingly remained in their company during the remaining thirteen days. The court further determined that the plaintiff's "volitional capacity prior to treatment may well have been impaired" (*id*. at 128):

> As such, we hold that when parents, or their agents, acting under the conviction that the judgmental capacity of their adult child is impaired, seek to extricate that child from what they reasonably believe to be a religious or pseudo-religious cult, and the child at some juncture assents to the actions in question, limitations upon the child's mobility do not constitute meaningful deprivations of personal liberty sufficient to support a judgment for false imprisonment. (*Id*. at 129)

With reference to the intentional infliction of emotional distress charge, the Minnesota Supreme Court upheld the trial court's admission of evidence concerning defendants' perceptions of The Way and their fears for Peterson's well-being. The court considered the defendants' claimed good faith to be a proper defense to punitive damages. It therefore found no violation of the first amendment admonition respecting freedom of religion in the admission of evidence bearing on the defendants' state of mind (*id*. at 129–30).

Weiss v. Patrick and *Peterson v. Sorlien* are not only exceptions to the general pattern, but are poor law as well. To show why, an analysis of an opinion occupying middle ground is in order. Judge Williams' opinion in *Baer v. Baer* (450 F.Supp. 481, N.D. Cal. 1978) has been widely cited in subsequent cases and law review articles. Its strengths lie in its thoroughness and eloquence; nonetheless, I believe the decision establishes an unfortunate precedent given the facts of the case and the possible avenues of redress. Baer's parents had sought and obtained appointment as conservator for their son, who was an adult member of the Unification Church. While Baer was walking with his parents, he was taken into custody by agents of the Freedom of Thought Foundation, assisted by local police. The typical deprogramming scenario began. In the aftermath, Baer alleged causes of action under sections 1983 and 1985(3), claiming deprivation of the rights to freedom of religion, association and speech; to due process and equal protection of the laws; to be secure in his person and property; to be let alone; and to travel freely (*id.* at 485).

Judge Williams determined that Baer had failed to state a cause of action under either section 1983 or 1985(3) and accordingly dismissed his complaint. On the 1983 cause, he ruled that the plaintiff had failed to allege that the private defendants and public officials had acted with a "common understanding or 'meeting of the minds'" (*id.* at 487–88). The defendants' resort to state courts was not sufficient to supply the necessary state action for maintenance of a 1983 cause of action:

> Such disinterested and indirect involvement by the state is too insignificant to bring the discrimination within the pale of constitutional prohibitions. (*Id.* at 486)

The conservatorship-granting judge was found to be judicially immune, and the police to have been carrying out a court order valid on its face (*id.* at 488).

Turning to the 1985(3) cause of action, the judge concluded that Baer had established the elements set forth in *Griffin*—in particular, that members of fringe or minority religious groups can suffer from "irrational and odious class discrimination akin to racial bias" (*id.* at 491). But Judge Williams refused to perceive a congressional source of authority to reach the conspiracy: Baer failed to show that he intended to travel interstate at the time of his kidnapping or that the conspirators intended to impair his right to do so (*id.* at 492). Nor was the judge willing to take the alternate thirteenth amendment route sanctioned in *Griffin*. Given uncertainty in the law and the absence of Supreme Court direction, he was unwilling to decide on his own that Congress had concluded that "the badges and incidents of slavery are borne by religious minorities as well as racial minorities" (*id.* at 493). Thus, he felt it would be unwise to hold that section 2 of the thirteenth amendment empowered Congress to fashion a civil remedy for private conspiracies denying freedom of religion (*id.*).

The *Baer* opinion is questionable in many respects. Other courts hearing cases of deprogrammed plaintiffs brought under sections 1983 and 1985(3) have been far more expansive, and, as a consequence, more compassionate to persons who are, after all, victims of violent crimes.

> We are not talking of minor children, but of adults. We are not talking of attempts merely to dispute and persuade, but of assault, kidnapping, capture, restraint, isolation, harrassment, vilification, and humiliation. (Gutman, *amicus curiae* brief in *Neale v. Pfeiffer*, No. 81-3523/3524, 6th Cir. 1981)

Even on the section 1983 cause of action, there may be significant doubt as to the wisdom of the *Baer* decision.

> Section 1983 was enacted to provide civil rights protection against official inaction and the states' toleration of private lawlessness. Thus, the *Baer* court's reliance on the state's disinterest to reject the plaintiff's section 1983 claim is misplaced; it is precisely a combination of a state's toleration and inaction that should invoke section 1983. (LaCava: 780)

Section 1983 contains language about governmental custom and usage; customs may be actions or inactions, and in the *Baer* case, an argument can be made that granting a conservatorship as a routine matter is both an official action and a failure of official action to maintain vigilance in the face of threats to rights of citizens (see *Monell v. Department of Social Services of the City of New York*, 436 U.S. 658, 1978, which liberalized access to the courts in section 1983 cases). If a state forum is misused in order to deny a person his constitutional liberties, then rights are being circumvented under color of law—the same sort of systematic action/inaction that was the case in the South during Reconstruction as far as our black racial minority was concerned (see LaCava: 780–82).

The *Baer* court, moreover, never inquired into the grounds for granting the conservatorship order in the first place, nor did it consider first amendment questions implicit in the underlying conservatorship proceeding. By refusing to take up the issue, "the court sanctioned the state's involvement in the indiscriminate kidnapping of those persons who become adherents of unpopular religious cults" (LaCava: 783).

The same comment should be made about Williams' very conservative opinion on Baer's 1985(3) complaint. Once having conceded that a religion may count as a class for 1985(3) purposes, and that the requisite discriminatory animus existed among the conspirators, the court's decision stopped cold and refused to grant a remedy. Several alternatives were available to the judge on the congressional source of authority issue, and to take the narrowest possible reading of the law and the facts of the case is tantamount to leaving religious minorities wholly without protection. Since the first amendment is incorporated into the fourteenth (Babbitt: 243), then the right to religious free exercise should be within the remedial jurisdiction of Congress, and protection of that right should be enforceable under section 5 of the fourteenth amendment. Unwilling to follow *Action* and *Westberry* in this regard, Judge Williams simply ducked the issue by deferring to the Supreme Court for guidance. Yet even if the *Baer* court was unwilling to take the risk of excessively expanding the enforcement powers of Congress directly over private acts, several less innovative possibilities were available. The most obvious was deprivation of the right to travel interstate. Whatever Baer's intentions at the time of his abduction, he was kidnapped while he was on a public street and then involuntarily detained. Forcible restraint obviously cuts off freedom of movement, and following *Griffin*, this fact alone should be sufficient to invoke a congressional source of power to protect a citizen's right to travel at liberty among the states. Fortunately, cases such as *Rankin* and *Ward*, as opposed to *Baer*, have set the precedents on this issue, so justice, rather than illiberal conceptions of judicial restraint, has been served in granting redress.

Still other alternatives remain. It might be possible, following *Jones v. Alfred H. Mayer Co.*, to rely on a thirteenth amendment rationale in the deprogramming cases. Forcible abduction and detention might then be looked upon as residual badges and incidents of slavery. Furthermore, "[b]oth the *Baer* and *Rankin* courts . . . might have concluded that the [Freedom of Thought] Foundation's interstate activities made it subject to the commerce clause" (LaCava: 787 n. 55) and a source of congressional power to reach private conspiracies found there.

The point about these technical legal suggestions is that a source of power to punish right-denying conspiracies in religious deprogramming cases should be found somewhere. An aura of blatant illegalities permeates all these cases. Basic religious liberties and the fundamental right to treatment as an equal are transgressed by distraught relatives and the deprogrammers they hire to abduct their offspring. If the criminal justice system were effective in dealing with these cases, then a few sentences to life imprisonment under kidnapping statutes would quickly quash the involuntary counterindoctrination business. As it is, sections 1983 and 1985(3) seem to be the only avenues of recourse available to victims of deprogramming. *Rankin, Ward, Taylor* and other decisions have recognized the right of deprogrammed plaintiffs to sue their kidnappers; since the acts of the latter are malicious and outrageous, both punitive and compensatory damages should be permitted. If deprogrammers confine their work to one state, perhaps blocking the plaintiff's ability to claim that he has been deprived of his right to interstate travel (LaCava: 791), then section 5 of the fourteenth amendment should be invoked. *Taylor v. Gilmartin* provides some potential relief though the decision requires extension and elaboration. If all the elements of a proper 1985(3) suit are in place, then not to find a proper congressional source of power to reach a conspiracy condones lawlessness and vigilantism, and ensures that fundamental rights of citizens will continue to be violated. Analogous circumstances in the South after the Civil War prompted Congress to pass the Enforcement Act and the Klan Act. For judges today to fail to utilize these acts is to fan flames of religious persecution and bigotry across the land, jeopardizing the liberties of all citizens, not just those of a very small number of new religious group members.

Chapter 10
Conservatorships for Deprogramming

Since the ratification of the fourteenth amendment in 1868, Americans have enjoyed protection against the state afforded by the due process clause of the fourteenth amendment: "nor shall any State deprive any person of life, liberty, or property without due process of law." Due process means adherence to rules and principles that have been established for the protection of private rights; it requires state governments to be regular and reliable in their treatment of citizens.

With the untrammeled growth of the mental health establishment in recent years—and the concomitant expansion of its claims—a change has occurred in the nature of conflicts between individuals and the state over loss of liberty through involuntary civil commitment. Courts have decided cases that provide guidance about the kinds of factual circumstances that may justify commitment and confinement of non-criminal citizens. They have also examined the role of psychiatric experts and elaborated procedural due process safeguards. Because involuntary commitment and conservatorships for deprogramming raise similar constitutional and policy concerns, a review of current civil commitment standards will place proposed conservatorship legislation in perspective.

Procedural protections in involuntary civil commitment proceedings include the rights to notice, to the assistance of counsel, and to a full adversarial hearing. Further protection is provided by requiring the state to prove that an individual requires care against his will.

The impact of civil commitment on a person cannot be disputed. Loss of income, deprivation of home comforts, family, and friends, and the stigma attached to being labeled insane and locked up are among the grave practical consequences of commitment. Moreover, many civil rights and privileges—the rights to vote, to make contracts, to marry, even to drive a car—may be abridged after a finding of mental illness or incompetency. And future opportunities are diminished perhaps even more than in cases of criminal conviction. As a federal court observed in *Lessard v. Schmidt* (349 F.Supp. 1078, E.D. Wis. 1972):

> Even a brief examination of the effects of civil commitment upon those judged mentally ill shows the importance of strict adherence to stringent procedural requirements and the necessity for narrow, precise standards. (*Id.* at 1088)

The crucial procedural protection is the state's burden of proving that a person is so mentally ill as to be unable to care for himself. As the Supreme Court declared in *O'Connor v. Donaldson* (422 U.S. 563, 1975):

> A finding of 'mental illness' alone cannot justify a State's locking a person up against his will and keeping him indefinitely in simple custodial confinement. Assuming that that term can be given a reasonably precise content and that the 'mentally ill' can be identified with reasonable accuracy, there is still no constitutional basis for confining such persons involuntarily if they are dangerous to no one and can live safely in freedom. (*Id.* at 575)

The Court continued that "the mere presence of mental illness does not disqualify a person from preferring his home to the comforts of an institution" (*id.*). Sick people who are not dangerous, who can care for themselves, and who prefer their home environments to an institution probably abound. A heavy burden of proof is placed on those who want to commit them—precommitment standards have become narrow and precise. That some treatment could be provided the sick person is not sufficient, for the right to refuse treatment has been recognized by the courts (see, *e.g.*, *Winters v. Miller*, 446 F.2d 65, 68–71, 2d Cir., *cert. denied*, 404 U.S. 985, 1971).

The state's police power to confine the criminally insane must be distinguished from its *parens patriae* power to confine the mentally ill. The latter power is narrowly circumscribed: only when an individual is so incapacitated that he cannot make his own evaluation of his situation may *parens patriae* power come into play (see Note, 87 Harv. L. Rev. at 1207–22). Although the state may claim authority to help an "insane" person, that person must be gravely disabled, and grave disability has been taken by the courts to mean impairment of ability to care for one's physical needs. A state may not confine a person "thought to need treatment and justify that deprivation of liberty solely by providing some treatment" (*O'Connor v. Donaldson*, 422 U.S. at 589, Burger, C.J., concurring). Because predicting another's behavior is difficult, suspected or alleged dangerousness is not sufficient to warrant civil commitment.

The federal district court opinion in *Lessard v. Schmidt* spelled out standards for involuntary civil commitment under a state's *parens patriae* power with depth and precision. An individual's potential to do harm to others must be great in order to "justify such a massive curtailment of liberty" (349 F.Supp. at 1093, quoting from *Humphrey v. Cady*, 405 U.S. 504, 509, 1972). An overt act or threat to do substantial harm should be required; mere speculation, even that of psychiatric experts, is insufficient. Proof by the preponderance of the evidence will not do. Rather, the court in *Lessard* assigned to the state the burden of proving "beyond a reasonable doubt all facts necessary to show that an individual is mentally ill and dangerous" (349 F.Supp. at 1095). Even then, commitment is not acceptable if there are less drastic means for achieving the objective. *Lessard* places on the person recommending involuntary commitment the burden of proving the availability of less restrictive alternatives, such as clinical day care or referral to a community mental health clinic; the burden of proving the investigation of alternatives; and the burden of proving why the alternatives were deemed unsuitable (*id.* at 1096). Procedural safeguards also extend to psychiatric interviews: the subject of a commitment proceeding cannot be forced to speak to a psychiatrist and statements made to a psychiatrist cannot be the basis of a commitment order unless given voluntarily after notice of the possible consequences (*id.* at 1101–2). Strict adherence to the rules of evidence is required; hearsay evidence is excluded unless admissible under an exception to the hearsay rule (*id.* at 1103).

In addition to procedural due process limitations, substantive due process protections also come into play when a state asserts its *parens patriae* power to hospitalize individuals against their will. There are "substantive constitutional limits on the states' power to deprive their citizens of liberty for paternal reasons" (Burgett: 259). Individuals have the right to treatment and the right to refuse treatment. They may also be entitled to periodic review of their cases with a view toward release from confinement. Furthermore, due process requires "that the nature and duration of commitment bear some reasonable relation to the purpose for which the individual is committed" (*Jackson v. Indiana*, 406 U.S. 715, 738, 1972). Some benefit must accrue to the confined person within a reasonable period of time, and any intrapsychic or interpersonal improvement must be judged from the perspective of the patient rather than from that of his observers. Thus a confined person has a substantive right to "net benefit." Continued commitment is unjustified if the patient asserts that the price of deprivation of freedom outweighs the benefit of treatment.

These due process protections point to the emergent distinction between mental illness and incapacity, which has to do with a person's alleged impaired ability to meet his own physical needs. The standards for civil commitment apply only in instances of incapacity, and as we have seen, the standards are stringent and continuing. By contrast, many states have broad and imprecise conservatorship or guardianship laws, making it relatively simple for a person involuntarily to come under the control of another for a period of time.

In 1977, the year the *Katz* case arose, the California legislature revised its conservatorship statute, deleting the "likely to be deceived by artful and designing persons" language (see Chapter 2). The current California statute makes inability to care for personal needs the sole criterion for appointment of a personal conservator. Historically, the exercise of *parens patriae* authority had been accompanied by a minimum of due process protection.

But recognizing that the strict procedural protections afforded subjects of civil commitment proceedings were not being given proposed conservatees, the California legislation provided tough procedural safeguards applicable in conservatorship proceedings. Thus if a distraught California parent petitions for a conservatorship in order to extricate his child from a despised religious group, the proposed conservatee must be present unless he is physically unable to attend. Moreover, the proposed conservatee has a right to appointed counsel (see Jones: 80–81).

By contrast to California, many states are considering measures designed to alleviate the "cult problem" by making conservatorships more accessible. These bills fly in the face of first and fourteenth amendment guarantees. They would in effect legalize deprogramming and insulate deprogrammers from the risk of incurring charges of kidnapping and forcible restraint.

The guardianship bill proposed in Kansas in 1982 is typical of these measures. Its language mirrors the Lasher "anti-conversion" bills passed by the New York legislature. Both Lasher bills were vetoed by New York Governor Hugh Carey as unconstitutional and unworkable. The Kansas measure provided for the appointment of a temporary guardian on a showing that a proposed ward "has undergone a substantial behavior change and lacks substantial capacity to make independent and informed decisions . . ." (H.R. 2688, 1982 Sess., Kansas). The following factors may be considered in determining whether substantial behavior change has occurred: (1) alteration of values and life-style; (2) blunted emotional responses; (3) regression to child-like behavior; (4) physical changes such as weight change, cessation of menstruation or perspiration, and diminished rate of beard growth; and (5) impairment of ability to make decisions. In determining whether a proposed ward lacks substantial capacity to make informed decisions, the court may consider whether lack of capacity resulted from "exposure to a systematic course of coercive persuasion," whose features include: (1) manipulation of the environment; (2) isolation from family and friends; (3) control over information and communication; (4) physical debilitation due to inadequate sleep, diet, and medical care, and overly long work hours; and (5) "reduction of decisional capacity through performance of repetitious tasks, lack of physical and mental privacy or intense peer pressure to induce feeling of guilt and anxiety, fear of the outside world, child-like dependency, a simplistic polarized view of reality or renunciation of self, family and previously held values" (id.). In addition, the Kansas bill requires both proof that the individuals conducting the course of the persuasion systematically misrepresent the true identity of the organization or the nature of its activities, and proof that the individuals conducting the course of the persuasion misled the proposed ward regarding the organization's identity and activities.

The language of conservatorship bills varies from state to state, but most follow the Lasher bills fairly closely. Their intent is plain: they are aimed at stigmatizing new religions and stemming their activities. For a prescribed period of time, the conservator becomes the "jailer, censor and dictator over all aspects of the individual's life" (Gutman, 1983).

> These bills share much in common. They share fuzziness of language, use of buzz words arising in ignorance and prejudice, lack of definition, and incorporation of vague and undefined scientific sounding phrases. They seek to base imposition of Draconian restrictions of liberty upon standards both vague and elusive. These bills would visit punishment upon an individual for exhibiting symptoms which the law finds undesirable and detrimental to the individual but allegedly having their genesis in practices and techniques alleged to have been engaged in by others. . . . [T]he conservatorship bills visit the punishment upon the 'victim.' (*Id.*)

Conservatorship bills aimed at converts to new religions in effect would impose a variety of civil commitment. But the measures do not provide the procedural and substantive due process safeguards afforded persons who are the subject of involuntary civil commitment proceedings. Medical stigmatization of membership in one or another new religious movements provides the impetus for consideration of these facially unconstitutional pieces of legislation. Proponents of the measures consider the behavior of a religious convert to be profoundly pathological, rather than the reflection of a change of mind. Stricken parents and sympathetic courts have not been slow to find support for this position in the psychiatric literature. A major new textbook in psychiatry contains an article on cults: cult membership by itself qualifies one for a psychiatric label according to Drs. Louis J. West and Margaret Singer (3250). "Victims" (members) undergo "traumatic neurosis" (they convert). They are "brainwashed" into membership. Dr. John Clark even calls this conversion and subsequent behavioral change "temporal lobe epilepsy" (quoted in Collins: 18). Groups are successful because they "induce trance" in order to change minds (West and Singer: 3250).

Wielding this kind of stigmatizing lingo, parents implore judges to impose conservatorships authorizing complete deprivation of the ward's liberty. At the same time, they by-pass the stringent due process standards governing involuntary civil commitment. If a proposed ward is indeed incapacitated, then compassion calls for a search for a cure. The right to treatment is recognized, but the right to refuse treatment is not because a ward under the care of a guardian is not free to do anything at all. He is literally a prisoner without legal recourse.

Violations of the Constitution occurred again and again throughout the 1970s. Conservatorships were perfunctorily granted and deprogramming was carried out under color of state authority. After the *Katz* decision, the situation changed. Fewer conservatorships were granted for deprogramming, but lawless vigilante-style deprogramming continued nonetheless, complete with all the frightening and humiliating assaults and kidnappings wreaked on members of new religious movements. Professional deprogrammers continued to bilk parents and relatives out of extraordinarily high fees. Moreover, they masked their failures by alleging that a post-deprogramming subject "floats" for a period of time; if the subject returned to the group, it was the parents' fault rather than the deprogrammer's.

The law and the judiciary have played a role in all of this. If fewer conservatorships for deprogramming have been granted since the *Katz* decision, the pressure on parents to take the law into their own hands has been heightened. Yet prosecutors and district attorneys have been loath to bring criminal actions against deprogrammers and especially against parents and relatives. The law has reached a kind of *de facto* detente with the forcible deprogramming business: it has allowed fewer before-the-fact conservatorships, but at the same time has refused to punish after-the-fact kidnappings and deprogrammings, even where clear cases of assault, battery, illegal restraint, and felony kidnapping charges could easily have been established. Perhaps something closely akin to judicial handling of euthanasia has been occurring. Judges may not allow disconnecting a person from life-sustaining equipment but, at the same time, they refuse to punish someone who in fact takes a life in extreme and hopeless medical circumstances.

Ironically, the post-*Katz* detente with extra-legal deprogramming has prompted one legal commentator to propose model guardianship legislation specifically designed to accommodate bereft families of new religious group members. Douglas Aronin correctly observes that public sympathy with the parents of cultists has resulted in sporadic enforcement of state laws proscribing extra-legal conduct; he suggests that cult members might receive better protection under a properly drawn guardianship statute (17 Colum. J.L. & Soc. Probs. at 273). Aronin is sensitive to the constitutional issues raised in granting guardianships for deprogramming. But his rationale is flawed: in his eagerness to redress what he perceives to be a major social problem, he stacks the deck in favor of families seeking to retrieve errant children from the clutches of new religious groups.

Aronin subscribes to the basic premises of the two Lasher bills passed by the New York legislature (*id.* at 234). But drawing upon lessons learned from Governor Carey's vetoes of the measures, he sets himself the task of drafting legislation that is both workable and constitutional (*id.* at 166). Thus the procedural due process protections incorporated in his model legislation are a substantial improvement upon the Lasher bills. Under Aronin's proposal, a guardianship order cannot issue upon a mere *ex parte* hearing. The proposed ward must be present both at the preliminary or "show cause" hearing and at the final hearing on the merits of the petition. Deprogramming is prohibited in the interim period between the preliminary and final hearings, although it seems questionable whether a petitioner awarded interim custody of a proposed ward would honor a promise not to engage in premature deprogramming. If the proposed ward is unable to attend the final hearing, a guardian *ad litem* may be appointed to protect his interests. The prospective ward is entitled to legal counsel, and the "cult" to which he belongs may intervene in the proceedings. The petitioner must establish the elements for issuance of a temporary guardianship order by clear and convincing evidence (*id.* at 247–63).

The real difficulties with Aronin's proposal lie in the substantive standards he adopts for imposition of a guardianship. His standards are riddled with assumptions about new religious movement conduct; he concedes that his model legislation "was drafted to deal with the paradigm of what cult opponents claim to be a typical cult encounter" (*id.* at 235). Analytically, Aronin's underlying but unstated first premise is that cults are socially undesirable. He betrays his bias when he declares that "the cult setting is one which an individual should enter only in the exercise of his free will" (*id.* at 217). The second premise follows: since no reasonable person would choose freely to associate with an undesirable outfit, something untoward must be going on in the recruitment and "indoctrination" of cult members (see *id.* at 168–75). That something untoward occurs in two stages. In the first stage, the cult engages in deception in the initial recruitment of new members (*id.* at 242). In the second, the cult practices "coercive persuasion" to indoctrinate members in the faith. Aronin defines coercive persuasion as follows in his model legislation:

> '[C]oercive persuasion' means a course of conduct in which an individual or group of individuals, with the intent or effect of depriving persons subject to such course of conduct of the ability or capacity to make independent decisions or to act in a voluntary manner, attempts to manipulate or control the environment of such persons through such means as isolation, control over information and channels of communication, physical debilitation or deprivation, intense peer pressure, lack of physical or mental privacy, abnormally long work schedules and continual performance of repetitious tasks, and other similar or related methods. (*Id.* at 275)

Like Richard Delgado, Aronin further assumes that coercive persuasion prevents cult recruits from being simultaneously able to possess both the knowledge and the capacity to give voluntary consent (*id.* at 199–200; 239). This assumption lays the foundation for his premise that deprivation of free will constitutes a "sufficiently compelling state interest to justify infringement on religious liberty" (*id.* at 212). He caps his sequence of assumptions by positing "that existing laws are inadequate to deal with the problems caused by cults, and that less intrusive remedies would be likewise inadequate" (*id.* at 233).

Aronin's assumptions appear in his model legislation in the form of statutory presumptions. In order to avoid defeating the purposes of the bill (*id.* at 234), he declines to require affirmative evidence that the proposed ward himself has been subject to coercive persuasion.

> The proposal instead permits a conclusive presumption that the individual has been subject to coercive persuasion upon proof of three facts; the cult normally practices coercive persuasion, the circumstances of the individual's involvement are such as to raise the reasonable inference that he has been subject to 'coercive persuasion,' and his current psychological state is such as might have resulted from 'coercive persuasion.' (*Id.* at 236)

Moreover, a petitioner need not prove that a cult intended to deprive a proposed ward of his free will; if the effects of coercive persuasion are present, intent may be presumed (*id.* at 238).

The model legislation properly places on the petitioner the burden of proving that the proposed ward lacks the capacity to make voluntary decisions. But similar sleights-of-hand are apparent here: Aronin assumes that the most relevant indication of incapacity is incapacity to decide whether to remain in the cult (*id.* at 242). Continuing devotion to the cult therefore becomes evidence of incapacity—a recruit would leave the cult if he could.

Aronin recognizes that no court has ever held that deprivation of the ability to exercise free will constitutes a compelling state interest (*id.* at 212). Nonetheless, he urges that the strong presumption in favor of religious liberty can be overcome by the state's interest in an individual's health and welfare. Thus we attain the therapeutic state, with intrusion on constitutionally protected religious belief justified by the assumption that cult membership connotes sickness.

The gravest problem with proposed conservatorship legislation is that it invites illegitimate inquiry into the nature or content of religious belief. Douglas Aronin claims that freedom of belief is not at issue if one assumes that a recruit's adherence to a cult is involuntary (*id.*). But even granting for the sake of argument that a cult has engaged in deception and coercive persuasion, it does not necessarily follow that a recruit's belief is entirely involuntary (see Chapter 2). Thus a judge hearing a conservatorship petition could be obliged to separate those elements of a person's belief that are coercively persuaded from those that are present by free and voluntary choice. Following the reasoning of the *Katz* appellate court, that separation cannot be accomplished without unconstitutionally trenching on the nature of a person's belief.

Legislatures must not cave in to public pressure to pass conservatorship bills aimed at the new religious movements. These measures overlook many of the procedural and substantive due process protections considered essential in civil commitment proceedings. Moreover, religious devotion may not "be used as the trigger for involuntary psychiatric treatment, nor can religious beliefs themselves be 'treated,' without burdening the individual's freedom of religion" (Shapiro: 769). Justice Brandeis' warning in his dissent in *Olmstead v. United States* (277 U.S. 438, 1928) is pertinent:

> Experience should teach us to be most on our guard to protect liberty when the government's purposes are beneficient. . . . The greatest dangers to liberty lurk in insidious encroachment by men of zeal, well-meaning but without understanding. (*Id.* at 479)

PART IV

Civil Liberties
and New Religious Movements

Chapter 11
The Cultivation of Individual Liberties

The preceding chapters have cautioned us to be mindful of the fragility of our individual liberties. In particular, they have urged the necessity of protecting the first and fourteenth amendment rights of members of new religious movements, lest the liberties of all of us be debased by acceding to majoritarian preferences. They have also shown that constitutional adjudication is a complex and continuing process, subject to vagaries of time, place, jurisprudential persuasion, and even prejudice. Repeatedly, the preceding chapters have warned of the danger of judicial innovation potentially curtailing the exercise of rights guaranteed by the Constitution.

A series of decisions by the Supreme Court in its 1982–83 term demonstrates that the warning was not without foundation. These decisions find the court in disarray, torn between constitutional principle and assertions of social policy. The Court is also divided by conflicting views of the role of the judiciary in protecting private rights. A majority of the current Court appears eager to shift responsibility for securing individual liberties to Congress and the states. But the Court is also at pains to reconcile its new-found reticence with the civil libertarian thrust of many decisions of the Warren Court and the early Burger Court.

Divisions within the Court are nowhere more apparent than in *United Brotherhood of Carpenters & Joiners Local 610 v. Scott* (103 S.Ct. 3352, 1983). *Scott* addressed the scope of 42 U.S.C. section 1985(3), and is the most significant construction of the conspiracy section of the Klan Act since the Court's 1971 decision in *Griffin v. Breckenridge* (see Chapter 8). New religious movement claims were not directly at issue. But it is necessary to discuss the decision in some detail, given the argument in previous chapters and the effect the decision may have upon subsequent 1985(3) actions brought by deprogrammed members of the new religions.

United Brotherhood of Carpenters v. Scott arose in the context of a labor dispute. A construction company had hired non-union workers for a Port Arthur, Texas, construction project. By prearrangement, protesting local union members drove to the construction site, assaulted non-union employees, and destroyed company equipment. The company and two employees who had been beaten filed an action in federal district court under section 1985(3), alleging a conspiracy to deprive them of constitutionally protected rights. The district court found that the elements of *Griffin v. Breckenridge* had been satisfied. The judge held that the union conspirators were motivated by a class-based, invidiously discriminatory animus, and that Congress had authority to reach the conspirators through the first amendment guarantee of freedom of association (103 S.Ct. 3355–56). The Fifth Circuit Court of Appeals affirmed.

The Supreme Court granted certiorari "[b]ecause of the importance of the issue involved" (*id.*). In a five-to-four decision, the Court reversed the fifth circuit. Writing for the majority, Justice White first considered whether Congress had authority under section 1985(3) to redress the injury caused by the union conspiracy to deny the non-union employees' rights. Following *Griffin v. Breckenridge*, he recognized that 1985(3) is not limited by the constraints of the fourteenth amendment. But because the section "'provides no substantial rights itself' to the class conspired against, . . . [t]he rights, privileges, and immunities that § 1985(3) vindicates must be found elsewhere . . ." (*id.* at 3358, quoting from *Great American Federal Savings & Loan Association v. Novotny*, 442 U.S. 366, 372, 1979). Since the right of association claimed by non-union employees in *Scott* had its source in the first amendment, Justice White looked to the language of that amendment to determine whether 1985 reached the union conspiracy.

> Because that Amendment restrains only official conduct, to make out their § 1985(3) case, it was necessary for respondents to prove that the state was somehow involved in or affected by the conspiracy. (103 S.Ct. at 3358)

In effect, the majority divided constitutional rights into two classes: those that are protected only against interference by government and those that are protected against both private and official encroachment. On its face, the first amendment falls in the former class, while the thirteenth amendment prohibition against slavery falls in the latter class. Thus section 1985(3) does not reach a conspiracy to infringe first amendment rights "unless it is proved that the state is involved in the conspiracy or that the aim of the conspiracy is to influence the activity of the state" (*id.* at 3357).

Justice White attempted to reconcile the majority's view with the Court's decision in *Griffin v. Breckenridge*. He conceded that the Court had held in *Griffin* that section 1985(3) reaches purely private conspiracies that in no way involve the state (*id.* at 3358). But according to Justice White:

> *Griffin* did not hold that even when the alleged conspiracy is aimed at a right that is by definition a right only against state interference the plaintiff in a § 1985(3) suit nevertheless need not

> prove that the conspiracy contemplated state involvement of
> some sort. The complaint in *Griffin* alleged, among other things,
> a deprivation of First Amendment rights, but we did not sustain
> the action on the basis of that allegation and paid it scant atten-
> tion. Instead, we upheld the application of § 1985(3) to private
> conspiracies aimed at interfering with rights constitutionally pro-
> tected against private, as well as official, encroachment. (*Id.*)

Having disposed of the source of authority issue, the Court turned to
the question whether section 1985(3) reaches conspiracies against workers who refuse to join a union. *Griffin*, it will be recalled, established the
requirement that conspirators be motivated by "some racial, or perhaps
otherwise class-based, invidiously discriminatory animus" (403 U.S. at
102). The *Scott* court of appeals had reasoned that political activities
were within the purview of the Klan Act, and had concluded that animus against non-union employees "was sufficiently similar to the animus
against a political party to satisfy the requirements of § 1985(3)" (103
S.Ct. at 3359).

Five members of the Supreme Court declared themselves "unper-
suaded."

> [I]t is a close question whether § 1985(3) was intended to reach any
> class-based animus other than animus against Negroes and those
> who championed their cause, most notably Republicans. (*Id.*)

Thus, even if the Klan Act could be construed to reach conspiracies
aimed at political classes, Justice White could find no warrant in the act's
legislative history to extend it "to reach conspiracies motivated by bias
towards others on account of their *economic* views, status, or activities"
(*id.* at 3360, emphasis in original). The Court once again raised the spec-
ter of federalization of tort law, and concluded that economic and com-
mercial conflicts are best resolved by recourse to federal or state statutes,
"as well as by the general law proscribing injuries to persons and property" (*id.* at 3361). Following the lead of *Griffin*, the majority declined
to specify which, if any, non-racial classes might qualify for protection
under section 1985(3). The Court's holding clearly excluded economic
classes. But its grudging reading of the legislative history of the Klan Act
seems destined further to restrict access to the remedy provided by the
Act's conspiracy section.

Justice Blackmun wrote the dissenting opinion, joined by Justices
Brennan, Marshall and O'Connor. He condemned the majority's rationale, finding "no basis for the Court's crabbed and uninformed reading
of the words of § 1985(3)" (103 S.Ct. at 3369). Addressing the first prong
of the majority opinion, Justice Blackmun declared:

> The Court . . . holds that § 1985(3) protects a private con-
> spiracy to interfere with the exercise of First Amendment rights

> only if some state action is involved. . . . The Court assumes that
> § 1985(3) merely bans private conspiracies to accomplish depriva-
> tions that are actionable under § 1983 when caused by state offi-
> cials. Although Congress could have passed such a statute, the
> simple fact is that it did not. (*Id.* at 3361–62; see also Chapter 9
> on the distinction between section 1983 and section 1985[3])

Justice Blackmun reviewed the legislative history of the Klan Act (see
Chapter 6), focusing particularly on the remarks of the moderate Republicans whose support insured passage of the measure.

> Throughout the debates on § 2, the Republican majority
> agreed that the Fourteenth Amendment conferred rights, includ-
> ing the right to equal protection of the laws, directly on persons
> and that those rights could be violated by private conspirators.
> The debate was over the conditions under which the Federal
> Government could step in to assert jurisdiction to protect those
> rights—a separate constitutional question of federal-state com-
> ity—not over the nature of the rights themselves. By limiting § 2
> to deprivation of equal protection and of equal privileges and
> immunities, the Forty-Second Congress avoided the constitutional
> problems the more moderate Republicans saw in the creation of a
> general federal criminal law. The effect of that language was to
> limit federal jurisdiction to cases in which persons were the
> victims of private conspiracies motivated by the intent to inter-
> fere in the equal exercise and enjoyment of their legal rights.
> Congress did not intend any requirement of state involvement in
> either a civil or criminal action under § 2. (*Id.* at 3365)

The dissenting opinion observed that the *Scott* majority had adopted
a requirement of state involvement virtually identical to that suggested
in *Collins v. Hardyman* (*id.* at 3366; see also Chapter 7). This requirement, Justice Blackmun commented, had been put to rest by the Court's
decision in *Griffin v. Breckenridge*. He accused the majority of ignoring
the fact that the *Griffin* Court had expressly rejected any requirement of
state involvement, even when the particular constitutional right implicated is one against state action (*id.*, n. 13, referring to 403 U.S. at 99).
He further accused the majority of confusing statutory construction with
constitutional interpretation.

> Determining the scope of § 1985(3) is a matter of statutory con-
> struction and has nothing to do with current interpretations of
> the First or Fourteenth Amendments. The Forty-Second Con-
> gress' view of its constitutional authority in 1871 to reach private
> conduct under the Fourteenth Amendment is relevant in inter-
> preting the reach of § 1985(3). (*Id.* at 3362 n. 3)

Justice Blackmun also rebutted the majority's holding that the non-
union employees in *Scott* did not constitute a protected class. In his
view, Congress intended a functional definition of the scope of section
1985(3).

> Congress intended to provide a federal remedy for all *classes* that seek to exercise their legal rights in unprotected circumstances similar to those of the victims of Klan violence. (*Id.* at 3367, emphasis in original)

Blackmun observed that Congress had demonstrated solicitude toward economic migrants, another group subject to Klan attack (*id.* at 3368). He concluded that the union members' conspiracy to keep Port Arthur a union-dominated town was similar to the Klan conspiracies Congress intended to punish in enacting section 1985(3) (*id.* at 3369). Thus he and the other dissenters could not countenance the majority's refusal to protect victims of a "classic case of mob violence intended to intimidate persons from exercising their legal rights" (*id.* at 3361).

The dissent in *United Brotherhood of Carpenters v. Scott* was correct in its construction of 1985(3), in its reading of the legislative history of the Klan Act, and in its interpretation of *Griffin v. Breckenridge*. The majority's constricted view of 1985(3) severely undercuts the Court's unanimous decision in *Griffin*. It leaves us with the formerly discredited *Collins v. Hardyman* rationale that state involvement must be shown in cases implicating constitutional rights negatively protected against governmental interference. (See Chester Antieau's observations on *Collins* in Chapter 7). The majority's error is the worse for ignoring the thrust of the Court's twelve-year-old opinion in *Griffin*—a thrust giving the Reconstruction period civil rights statutes "'a sweep as broad as [their] language'" (*Griffin v. Breckenridge*, 403 U.S. at 97, quoting *United States v. Price*, 383 U.S. 787, 801, 1966; see also, *Scott*, 103 S.Ct. at 3369).

There are two ways in which the Court's decision in *Scott* potentially affects deprogrammed members of new religions who seek to vindicate their constitutional rights by recourse to section 1985(3). First, the religious group to which the deprogrammed plaintiff belongs will be subjected to intensified scrutiny to determine whether it constitutes a protected class. The Court in *Scott* did not foreclose the imposition of liability on conspirators motivated by animus against religious affiliation. But the majority was loath to extend the reach of section 1985(3) beyond conspiracies motivated by racial bias. It remains to be seen how chilling an effect Justice White's language will have on access to the Klan Act's conspiracy remedy. The circuit court opinions in *Rankin v. Howard*, *Ward v. Connor*, and *Taylor v. Gilmartin* (see Chapter 9) still appear to afford the possibility of redress to deprogrammed members of new religions. The Supreme Court chose not to grant certiorari in any of these cases; it might have done so had it questioned deprogramming victims' eligibility for 1985(3) protection.

Deprogrammed plaintiffs seeking to avail themselves of the section 1985(3) remedy are also potentially affected by the *Scott* majority view of Congressional authority to reach right-denying conspiracies. Lower courts have been divided on the source of authority issue (see Chapters 8 and 9). A few courts have accepted the invitation in *Griffin v. Breckenridge* to reach wholly private conspiracies on the strength of the enforcement clause of the fourteenth amendment. Most courts have been more wary, preferring to rely either upon deprivations of the right to travel, or upon deprivations of rights protected against governmental interference that somehow implicate the state. The majority opinion in *Scott* unequivocally forecloses the former option. Thus section 1985(3) plaintiffs must prove that a conspiracy deprived them of rights specifically protected against private encroachment or that a conspiracy involving or influencing the state deprived them of rights specifically protected only against governmental interference.

Assuming that members of a particular new religious group constitute a protected class, the *Scott* result may not differ significantly from the results in *Rankin*, *Ward*, and *Taylor*. But even if the *Scott* decision does not vary the practice of lower courts in deciding the source of authority issue, for the moment it precludes further exploration of possibilities opened by the Court in *Griffin v. Breckenridge*. This kind of recision is also apparent in a number of other recent Supreme Court decisions affecting enforcement of first and fourteenth amendment rights.

In *Briscoe v. Lahue* (103 S.Ct. 1108, 1983), the Court held that 42 U.S.C. section 1983 did not authorize a convicted criminal defendant to assert a claim for damages against a police officer for giving perjured testimony at his trial. The majority declared:

> [I]t has been settled that the all-encompassing language of § 1983, referring to '[e]very person' who, under color of law, deprives another of federal constitutional or statutory rights, is not to be taken literally. (*Id.* at 1113, referring to *Tenney v. Brandhove*, 341 U.S. 367, 1951)

Three justices dissented in *Briscoe*. Justice Marshall attacked the majority's conclusion that Congress did not intend to abrogate common law witness immunity in section 1983 actions (103 S.Ct. at 1126). Joined by Justices Brennan and Blackmun, he further condemned the majority's resort to public policy considerations.

> The majority's primary concern appears to be that § 1983 suits against police witnesses would impose 'significant burdens on the judicial system and on law enforcement resources.' (*Id.* at 1132, quoting from *id.* at 1120)

Justice Marshall could "not conceive in this case how patent violations of individual rights can be tolerated in the name of the public good." He quoted from Chief Justice John Marshall's opinion in *Marbury v. Madison*:

'The very essence of civil liberty consists in the right of every individual to claim the protection of the laws, whenever he receives an injury.' (103 S.Ct. at 1133, quoting from 5 U.S. [1 Cranch] 137, 163, 1803)

The Court was again closely divided in *Connick v. Myers* (103 S.Ct. 1684, 1983), another action brought under section 1983. A majority of five justices determined that the first amendment was not violated by the discharge of an assistant district attorney who had distributed a questionnaire to her fellow employees eliciting information concerning working conditions in the office. The majority found that the assistant district attorney was speaking principally to matters of personal, rather than public, concern. The limited first amendment interest involved did not require the employer to tolerate action that he reasonably believed would disrupt the office, destroy working relationships and undermine his authority (*id.* at 1694). Four justices dissented, asserting that speech about the manner in which the government is operated is an essential part of communications necessary for self-governance (*id.* at 1697, Brennan, J., dissenting). The dissenters further attacked the majority's conclusion that the state's interest in a smoothly running district attorney's office outweighed the discharged employee's first amendment right to freedom of speech (*id.* at 1701–2).

A five-justice majority similarly denigrated first amendment rights in *Perry Education Association v. Perry Local Educators' Association* (103 S.Ct. 948, 1983). The Court held that the free speech clause was not violated by granting an incumbent teachers' union access to the interschool mail system, while denying access to a rival union. Writing for the majority, Justice White found that the mail system was not a public forum, and that distinctions based on status were therefore permissible (*id.* at 957). The four dissenters countered that granting exclusive access to the incumbent union amounted to viewpoint discrimination infringing on the rival union members' first amendment rights (*id.* at 966, Brennan, J., dissenting). Moreover, the dissenters were not persuaded that the exclusive access policy advanced any substantial state interest (*id.* at 969).

In *Mueller v. Allen* (103 S.Ct. 3062, 1983), the Court considered whether a Minnesota statute allowing taxpayers to deduct expenses incurred for education of their children violated the establishment clause of the first amendment. In effect, the deduction subsidized tuition payments to sectarian schools. In another five-to-four decision, the Court held that the statute did not offend the prohibition against establishment of religion. Justice Rehnquist declared for the majority that the Minnesota legislature's judgment was "entitled to substantial deference" (*id.* at 3067). He characterized the financial benefits flowing to parochial schools as "attenuated," and belittled the risk of religious or denominational control over democratic processes (*id*. at 3069). He declined to engage in empirical inquiry into who was benefited by the statute, and without more, held that the deduction satisfied the "primary effect inquiry" of previous establishment clause cases (*id*. at 3071; see also Chapter 1).

The four dissenters in *Mueller* censured the majority's cavalier treatment of establishment clause precedent.

> For the first time, the Court has upheld financial support for religious schools without any reason at all to assume that the support will be restricted to the secular functions of those schools and will not be used to support religious instruction. This result is flatly at odds with the fundamental principle that a State may provide no financial support whatsoever to support religion. (*Id*. at 1078, Marshall, J., dissenting)

Justice Marshall was particularly critical of the majority's unconvincing effort to distinguish *Committee for Public Education v. Nyquist* (413 U.S. 756, 1973), which forbade financial aid to parents of parochial school students.

> The majority incorrectly asserts that Minnesota's tax deduction for tuition expenses 'bears less resemblance to the arrangement struck down in *Nyquist* than it does to assistance programs upheld in our prior decisions and discussed with approval in *Nyquist*.' . . . One might as well say that a tangerine bears less resemblance to an orange than to an apple. (103 S.Ct. at 3076, quoting from *id*. at 3066)

It may be true, as Justice Rehnquist observed in his majority opinion, that "the Establishment Clause presents especially difficult questions of interpretation and application" (*id*. at 3065). The majority justices in *Mueller* strained to reach what they considered the proper result, thereby compromising existing precedent and rendering interpretation of the establishment clause even more difficult.

One further case decided in the 1982–83 term warrants discussion here. In *Marsh v. Chambers* (103 S.Ct. 3330, 1983), the Court reviewed an establishment clause challenge to the Nebraska legislature's practice of opening each legislative day with a prayer by a chaplain paid by the state. The same Presbyterian minister had served as chaplain for sixteen years. A majority of six justices upheld the practice on historical grounds. Chief Justice Burger wrote for the Court:

> In light of the unambiguous and unbroken history of more than 200 years, there can be no doubt that the practice of opening legislative sessions with prayer has become part of the fabric of our society. To invoke Divine guidance on a public body entrusted with making the laws is not, in these circumstances, an 'establishment' of religion or a step toward establishment; it is

> simply a tolerable acknowledgment of beliefs widely held among the people of this country. (*Id.* at 3336)

The Court was satisfied that the history of legislative prayer gave "abundant assurance that there is no real threat 'while this Court sits'" (*id.* at 3337, quoting from *Panhandle Oil Co. v. Mississippi ex rel. Knox*, 277 U.S. 218, 223, 1928, Holmes, J., dissenting).

Justice Brennan filed a long, thoughtful and scholarly dissent. He observed that the majority of the Court had not bothered to apply settled establishment clause doctrine laid down in *Lemon v. Kurtzman* (see Chapter 1), but had simply carved out an exception for legislative prayer from the first amendment prohibition against establishment of religion (103 S.Ct. at 3337–38). "Simply put, the Court seems to regard legislative prayer as at most a *de minimis* violation, somehow unworthy of our attention" (*id.* at 3349). Justice Brennan recognized that striking down legislative prayer would likely provoke a "furious reaction" (*id.* at 3351), but he felt the Constitution compelled precisely that result.

> Legislative prayer clearly violates the principles of neutrality and separation that are embedded within the Establishment Clause. . . . It intrudes on the right to conscience by forcing some legislators either to participate in a 'prayer opportunity,' . . . with which they are in basic disagreement, or to make their disagreement a matter of public comment by declining to participate. It forces all residents of the State to support a religious exercise that may be contrary to their own beliefs. It requires the State to commit itself on fundamental theological issues. It has the potential for degrading religion by allowing a religious call to worship to be intermeshed with a secular call to order. And it injects religion into the political sphere by creating the potential that each and every selection of a chaplain, or consideration of a particular prayer, or even reconsideration of the practice itself, will provoke a political battle along religious lines and ultimately alienate some religiously identified group of citizens. (*Id.* at 3344)

Brennan further recognized that tensions inherent in the role of religion and religious belief in a free society mandate occasional deviation from absolute adherence to separation and neutrality (*id.*; see also Chapter 1). But for him, this was not a case in which competing first amendment interests required variance from principle. Thus, even though abolishing legislative prayer would have proved unpopular, he was convinced that doing so would have "invigorated both the 'spirit of religion' and the 'spirit of freedom'" (*id.* at 3351).

Justice Brennan's concluding remarks in *Marsh v. Chambers* underscore developing factionalism within the Court. As the preceding cases from the 1982–83 term demonstrate, a narrow majority seems willing to elevate expediential policy concerns over constitutional principle. In *United Brotherhood of Carpenters v. Scott*, the Court invoked the bugbear of federalization of tort law in order to justify limiting access to the remedy for conspiratorial deprivation of rights afforded by section 1985(3). In *Briscoe v. Lahue*, the majority immunized police witnesses from suit under section 1983 because of reluctance to impose further burdens on law enforcement officials and on the judiciary. In *Connick v. Myers* and *Perry Education Association*, the Court gave work-place concerns priority over the right to free speech. And in *Mueller v. Allen* and *Marsh v. Chambers*, deference to legislative judgment and tradition took precedence over the prohibition against establishment of religion.

These decisions may find popular support, but they represent judicial abdication of responsibility for preservation of private rights. Something akin to what occurred in the wake of Reconstruction may be occurring in the Court today. Now, as then, the Court's readings seem to reflect weariness and disenchantment with assertions of civil liberties. In both times, the ultimate consequence has been retraction of protections previously thought to have been guaranteed by the Constitution and implementing statutes enacted by Congress. Weariness and disenchantment cannot be equated with disdain, but the result is the same: Constitutional rights are demeaned and the means for vindicating them are eroded. The majority defends this result by imprecating the public good, but fails to recognize that policy concerns necessarily are of a lesser order than private rights (see Chapter 5).

The Court's current willingness to favor its perceptions of the public good over principle does not bode well for members of the new religions seeking to redress violations of their constitutional rights. Prejudice against cults is pervasive (see Chapters 4 and 5). Many people seem to view conversion to a new religion as a betrayal of family and a renunciation of right-thinking allegiances and values. For these people, something must be wrong when a child—even an adult child—spurns nurture and embraces instead an exotic and all-consuming religious belief. Social discomfiture is manifest in judicial treatment of parental petitions for conservatorships to deprogram cult adherents. For the superior court judge who granted the temporary conservatorship orders in *Katz*, mother, father and children were the "very essence of life" and civilization (quoted at 73 Cal. App. 3d at 963 n. 8, 141 Cal. Rptr. at 240 n. 8). Similarly, the probate judge who imposed the guardianship in *Taylor v. Gilmartin* assigned more weight to parental concerns than to an adult child's right to be free from temporary custody (see 686 F.2d at 1349). Proposed conservatorship legislation designed to assist parents in retrieving children from cults likewise serves an apparently primordial social interest in preservation of the family (see Chapter 10). This fundamental social interest does not enjoy explicit constitutional protection, but is buttressed by claims of coercive persuasion and emergency. Thus, parents and other interested persons call upon the state to assert its *parens patriae* authority over individuals in the name of the integrity of the family. When the courts accede to this bootstrapping exercise, they jeopardize the right to religious autonomy and the even more basic right to treatment as an equal.

The social interest in domestic tranquility may not be used to justify abridgment of fundamental rights, particularly when arguments favoring abridgment are erected upon prejudice or an exaggerated account of emergency. The moral right to equality was made a legal right in religious matters by the first and fourteenth amendments and also, as we have seen, by the Civil Rights Acts. These rights do not heed the whim of democratic majorities. Rather, they are rights that individuals hold even when the majority of citizens is convinced that society is worse off for allowing groups like the Alamo Foundation or Love Israel or the New Testament Missionary Fellowship to operate in our midst. These rights hold as well when our children join what are wisely perceived to be grotesque and harmful outfits. Society may well be worse off for allowing these things to happen, and grief and distress among families broken up by a child's defection are difficult to ignore. But whatever we may speculate about social and familial well-being, conservatorships for deprogramming and forcible deconversion are profound insults to religious freedom and to the fundamental right of being treated as an equal. As Ronald Dworkin argues:

> Laws that recognize and protect common interests, like laws against violence and monopoly, offer no insult to any class or individual; but laws that constrain one man, on the sole ground that he is incompetent to decide what is right for himself, are profoundly insulting to him. They make him intellectually and morally subservient to the conformists who form the majority and deny him the independence to which he is entitled. (1977:263)

The Constitution protects against the persecution of minorities. Regardless of majoritarian preferences, the state may not prefer one sort of group membership—especially religious affiliation—over another. We are committed to absolute freedom of belief and, absent a compelling, countervailing secular interest, to tolerating activities stemming from religious belief. Free exercise means that citizens are free to believe in and peddle mental and spiritual poison as long as they do so within the law (see Chapter 1).

In his dissent in *Adamson v. California* (322 U.S. 46, 1947), Justice Black drew upon the celebrated case of Anne Hutchinson, who was banished from the Massachusetts Bay Colony in 1637 for her unorthodox religious beliefs. He commented on the enduring nature of religious prejudice:

> People with a consuming belief that their religious convictions
> must be forced on others rarely ever believe that the unorthodox
> have any rights which should or can be rightfully respected. (*Id.*
> at 88)

In Justice Black's view, Mrs. Hutchinson's experience had "contributed to
the overwhelming sentiment that demanded adoption of a Constitutional
Bill of Rights" (*id.* at 88–89). However abstract, constitutional liberties
were designed to meet "human evils that have emerged from century to
century . . ." (*id.* at 89).

> [T]he people of no nation can lose their liberty so long as a Bill of
> Rights like ours survives and its basic purposes are conscientiously
> interpreted, enforced and respected so as to afford continuous
> protection against old, as well as new, devices and practices
> which might thwart those purposes. (*Id.*)

It is much easier to pay tribute to individual liberties than it is to
secure them in practice. Constitutional principle is demanding: to be
true to rights, we must cast aside prejudice and predilection even when
it is painful to do so. Cases involving members of the new religious
movements are hard cases because principle insists that we afford protection to unorthodox beliefs and practices that may offend a majority of
citizens.

As Justice Brennan recognized in his dissent in *Marsh v. Chambers*,
the "'spirit of religion' and the 'spirit of freedom'" require unpopular
decisions (103 S.Ct. at 3351). We may not be able to rely upon a majority of the current Supreme Court to make those decisions. Cases from
the 1982–83 term suggest that we may be entering upon another period
in which the Court is less than vigilant in performing its fiduciary obligation to protect private rights. But judicial reticence does not excuse the
rest of us. Citizens who are not judges lack formal power to interpret
and enforce the Constitution, but as we have seen, they can and do influence the course of constitutional adjudication. At the least, we owe it to
ourselves to cultivate our individual liberties and to make a sustained
and forceful argument on their behalf. We are at once the grantors and
the beneficiaries of the Constitution, and we cannot afford lapses in our
protection against devices and practices that thwart the basic purposes of
our trust.

NOTE ON CITATION

The social sciences citation format used in this book places references in parentheses within the sentence in which authorities are referred to or quoted. Since many of the authorities relied upon are judicial decisions or law review articles, it has been necessary to modify legal citation style to conform to the social sciences format. For example, legal convention prescribes the following citation style for a United States Supreme Court case:

Griffin v. Breckenridge, 403 U.S. 88 (1971).

But within the text of this book, the same Supreme Court case is cited in the following manner:

Griffin v. Breckenridge (403 U.S. 88, 1971).

In either instance, the initial numerals refer to the volume of United States Reports in which the case is reported. The second set of numerals refers to the page within the volume on which the report of the case begins. The final set of numbers indicates the year in which the case was decided.

When referring to legal materials, I have also utilized the "*id.*" form common to legal practice, but again in a modified social scientific style. *Id.* refers the reader to the immediately preceding citation, and obviates the need to cite it in full. Thus a quotation from *Griffin v. Breckenridge* might be cited as follows, with the numerals referring to the page or pages within the decision on which the quote appears:

(*Id.* at 102–3).

For the reader otherwise unfamiliar with reports of legal decisions, United States Supreme Court decisions that have not yet been printed in United States Reports (U.S.) are cited to the Supreme Court Reporter (S.Ct.).

Mueller v. Allen (103 S.Ct. 3062, 1983).

Decisions of the circuit courts of appeal are printed in the Federal Reporter, first or second series (F. or F.2d respectively). The circuit in which the case was decided is also cited.

United States v. Patrick (532 F.2d 142, 9th Cir. 1976).

Earlier circuit court decisions are reported in Federal Cases (F. Cas.) and include the circuit district as well as the cause number.

United States v. Given (25 F. Cas. 1324, C.C.D. Del. 1873, No. 15,210).

Federal district court opinions appear in the Federal Supplement (F. Supp.) and similarly refer to the district in which the case was decided.

Baer v. Baer (450 F. Supp. 481, N.D. Cal. 1978).

Decisions of state courts of record are reported in a variety of forms. Most states still publish official reports of their appellate court decisions. In addition, West Publishing Company prints unofficial reports from every American jurisdiction. For example, opinions from state courts of record in Alaska, Arizona, California, Colorado, Hawaii, Idaho, Kansas, Montana, Nevada, New Mexico, Oklahoma, Oregon, Utah, Washington and Wyoming are published in West's Pacific Reporter, first or second series (P. or P.2d), while opinions from Illinois, Indiana, Massachusetts, New York and Ohio are published in the North Eastern Reporter, first or second series (N.E. or N.E.2d). Because of the volume of appellate case law generated in New York and California, West offers separate reporters for decisions from those states. Thus *Katz v. Superior Court*, a decision of an intermediate California appellate court, is cited first to the official reporter (Cal. App. 3d) and then to the West reporter (Cal. Rptr.).

(73 Cal. App. 3d 952, 141 Cal. Rptr. 234, 1977).

Some states no longer publish official reports. For example, *Peterson v. Sorlien*, a decision of the Minnesota Supreme Court, is cited only to West's North Western Reporter, second series (N.W.2d).

(299 N.W.2d 123, Minn. 1980).

All cases referred to in the book are cited according to legal convention in the Table of Cases.

TABLE OF AUTHORITIES

Anthony, Dick
1979–80   "The Fact Pattern Behind the Deprogramming Controversy: An Analysis and an Alternative." In *Alternative Religions: Government Control and the First Amendment. New York University Review of Law and Social Change* 9:73–89.

Antieau, Chester J.
1971   *Federal Civil Rights Acts: Civil Practice.* Rochester, New York: Lawyers Cooperative Publishing Company.

Aronin, Douglas
1982   "Cults, Deprogramming, and Guardianship: A Model Legislative Proposal." *Columbia Journal of Law and Social Problems* 17:163–286.

Avins, Alfred
1967   "The Ku Klux Klan of 1871: Some Reflected Light on State Action and the Fourteenth Amendment." *St. Louis University Law Journal* 11:331–81.
1968   "Federal Power to Punish Individual Crimes under the Fourteenth Amendment: The Original Understanding." *Notre Dame Lawyer* 43:317–43.

Babbitt, Ellen M.
1979   "The Deprogramming of Religious Sect Members: A Private Right of Action Under Section 1985(3)." *Northwestern Law Review* 74:229–54.

Bromley, David G.
1979   "Atrocity Tales, the Unification Church, and the Social Construction of Evil." *Journal of Communication* 29, Summer: 42–53.

Bromley, David G., and Shupe, Anson D., Jr.
1981   *Strange Gods: The Great American Cult Scare.* Boston: Beacon.

Bromley, David G., and Richardson, James T., eds.
1983   *The Brainwashing/Deprogramming Controversy.*
            Toronto: Edwin Mellen Press.

Brophy, James E., III
1973   "The Troubled Waters of 1985(3) Litigation." *Law and the Social Order* 1973:639–78.

Buchanan, G. Sidney
1975   "Through the Looking Glass: The Thirteenth Amendment's Backward Trip through Time." *Houston Law Review* 12:331–78.

Burgett, David W.
1981   "Substantive Due Process Limits on the Duration of Civil Commitment for the Treatment of Mental Illness." *Harvard Civil Rights-Civil Liberties Law Review* 16:205–64.

Burkholder, John Richard
1974   "'The Law Knows No Heresy': Marginal Religious Movements and the Courts." In *Religious Movements in Contemporary America*, edited by Irving I. Zaretsky and Mark P. Leone. Pp. 27–50. Princeton: Princeton University Press.

Calkins, William D.
1972   "Civil Rights—Expansion of Remedies under 42 U.S.C. Section 1985(3): *Action v. Gannon.*" *Missouri Law Review* 37:525–31.

Coleman, James S.
1956   "Social Cleavage and Religious Conflict." *Journal of Social Issues* 12, No. 3:44–66.

Coleman, Lee
1982   "New Religions and 'Deprogramming': Who's Brainwashing Whom?" Typescript.
1984   *The Reign of Error: Psychiatry, Authority and Law.* Boston: Beacon. In Press.

Coleman, Lee, and Solomon, Trudy
1976   "Parens Patriae 'Treatment': Legal Punishment in Disguise." *Hastings Constitutional Law Quarterly* 3:345–62.

Collins, Glen
1982 "The Reasons 'Normal' Kids Fall for Cults." *San Francisco Chronicle*, March 23, 1982:18.

Cox, Archibald
1966 "The Supreme Court 1965 Term—Forward: Constitutional Adjudication and the Promotion of Human Rights." *Harvard Law Review* 80:91–122.
1968 *The Warren Court: Constitutional Decision as an Instrument of Reform.* Cambridge: Harvard University Press.
1981 *Freedom of Expression.* Cambridge: Harvard University Press.
1981 "Don't Overrule the Court." *Newsweek*, September 28, 1981:18.

Cuddihy, John Murray
1978 *No Offense: Civil Religion and Protestant Taste.* New York: New Seabury.

Davis, J. Michael
1976 "Brainwashing: Fact, Fiction and Criminal Defense." *University of Missouri Kansas City Law Review* 44:438–79.

Delgado, Richard
1977 "Religious Totalism: Gentle and Ungentle Persuasion under the First Amendment." *Southern California Law Review* 51:1–98.
1979–80 "Religious Totalism as Slavery." In *Alternative Religions: Government Control and the First Amendment. New York University Review of Law and Social Change* 9:51–67; 71.
1981 "New Religious Movements in the Courts: An Overview." Typescript.
1982 "Awaiting the Verdict on Recruitment." *The Center Magazine* 15, No. 2:25–29.
1982 "Cults and Conversion: The Case for Informed Consent." *Georgia Law Review* 16:533–74.

Dworkin, Ronald
1977 *Taking Rights Seriously.* Cambridge: Harvard University Press.
1979 "How to Read the Civil Rights Act." *The New York Review of Books*, December 20, 1979:37–43.

Edwards, Christopher
    1979   *Crazy for God: The Nightmare of Cult Life by an Ex-Moon Disciple*. Englewood Cliffs: Prentice-Hall.

Estreicher, Samuel
    1974   "Federal Power to Regulate Private Discrimination: The Revival of the Enforcement Clauses of the Reconstruction Era Amendments." *Columbia Law Review* 74:449–527.

Fiss, Owen, and Krauthammer, Charles
    1982   "The Rehnquist Court." *The New Republic*. March 10, 1982:14–21.

Fockele, Mark
    1979   "A Construction of Section 1985(c) in Light of Its Original Purpose." *Chicago Law Review* 46:402–42.

Frantz, Laurent B.
    1964   "Congressional Power to Enforce the Fourteenth Amendment against Private Acts." *Yale Law Journal* 73:1353–84.

Gutman, Jeremiah S.
    1977   "Constitutional and Legal Dimensions of Deprogramming." In *Deprogramming: Documenting the Issue*, edited by Herbert Richardson. Typescript distributed by the American Civil Liberties Union and the Toronto School of Theology.
    1979–80   "Extemporaneous Remarks." In *Alternative Religions: Government Control and the First Amendment. New York University Review of Law and Social Change* 9:69–71.
    1981   "Brief *Amicus Curiae* of Holy Spirit Association for the Unification of World Christianity, Inc.," in *Neale v. Pfeiffer*, No. 81/3523/3524, 6th Circuit, September 8, 1981.
    1985   "The Legislative Assault on New Religious Movements." In *Cults, Culture, and the Law: Perspectives on New Religious Movements*, edited by William C. Shepherd, Thomas Robbins, and James McBride. Chico: Scholars Press.

Hall, Elizabeth
    1981   "The Parent Battle Against the Cults is Heating Up." *San Francisco Chronicle*, November 9, 1981:16, 19.

Howe, Mark De Wolfe
1965   *The Garden and the Wilderness: Religion and Gov-
            ernment in American Constitutional History.* Chi-
            cago: University of Chicago Press.

Jones, Vreeland O.
1977   "Probate Code Conservatorships: A Legislative Grant
            of New Procedural Protections." *Pacific Law Journal*
            8:73–98.

Kelley, Dean
1977   "Deprogramming—What's Going On Here?" In *De-
            programming: A Book of Documents*, edited by
            Anne Pritchard. New York: American Civil Liberties
            Union:3–23.

Kittrie, Nicholas N.
1971   *The Right to be Different: Deviance and Enforced
            Therapy.* Baltimore: Johns Hopkins Press.

Kriedman, M. Ronald
1972   "Constitutional and Jurisdictional Problems in the
            Application of 42 U.S.C. § 1985(3)." *Boston Univer-
            sity Law Review* 52:599–621.

LaBarre, Weston
1969   *They Shall Take Up Serpents: Psychology of the
            Southern Snake-Handling Cult.* New York: Schocken.

LaCava, John J.
1979   "Federal Statutory Remedy Rejected for Religious
            Kidnapping Victim: *Baer v. Baer.*" *Connecticut Law
            Review* 11:773–91.

LeMoult, John
1978   "Deprogramming Members of Religious Sects." *Ford-
            ham Law Review* 46:599–640.

Levine, Mark G.
1974   "The Free Exercise Clause as a Defense to Involun-
            tary Civil Commitment: Bringing Mental Illness into
            Religion." *Albany Law Review* 39:144–56.

Lifton, Robert Jay
1961   *Thought Reform and the Psychology of Totalism: A
            Study of "Brainwashing" in China.* New York: Norton.

Malpass, Susan C.
1976   "Civil Rights—State Action is a Requirement for the Application of Section 1985(3) to First Amendment Rights." *North Carolina Law Review* 54:677–85.

Miller, Richard W.
1981   "Rights and Reality." *The Philosophical Review* 90, No. 3:383–407.

Note
1965   "Federal Civil Action Against Private Individuals for Crimes Involving Civil Rights." *Yale Law Journal* 74:1462–71.

Note
1974   "Civil Commitment of the Mentally Ill." *Harvard Law Review* 87:1190–1406.

Note
1977   "The Scope of Section 1985(3) Since *Griffin v. Breckenridge*." *George Washington Law Review* 45:239–59.

Note
1978   "Conservatorships and Religious Cults: Divining a Theory of Free Exercise." *New York University Law Review* 53:1247–89.

Note
1980   "The Class-Based Animus Requirement of 42 U.S.C. § 1985(c): A Suggested Approach." *Minnesota Law Review* 64:635–67.

Patrick, Ted
1976   *Let Our Children Go*. New York: Dutton.
1979   "Interview." *Playboy*, March, 1979.

Pfeffer, Leo
1967   *Church, State and Freedom*. Boston: Beacon.
1974   "The Legitimation of Marginal Religions in the United States." In *Religious Movements in Contemporary America*, edited by Irving I. Zaretsky and Mark P. Leone. Pp. 9–26. Princeton: Princeton University Press.

Pole, J. R.
1978   *The Pursuit of Equality in American History*. Berkeley and Los Angeles: University of California Press.

Pritchard, Anne, ed.
1977   *Deprogramming: A Book of Documents.* New York: American Civil Liberties Union.
1978   "Deprogramming and the Law." *ACLU Reports.* New York: American Civil Liberties Union.

Rawls, John
1972   *A Theory of Justice.* Cambridge: Harvard University Press.

Richardson, Herbert, ed.
1977   *Deprogramming: Documenting the Issue.* Typescript distributed by the American Civil Liberties Union and the Toronto School of Theology.

Robbins, Thomas
1979–80   "Religious Movements, the State, and the Law: Reconceptualizing 'The Cult Problem.'" In *Alternative Religions: Government Control and the First Amendment. New York University Review of Law and Social Change* 9:33–49.
1981   "Church, State, and Cult." *Sociological Analysis* 42:209–26.

Robbins, Thomas, and Anthony, Dick
1982   "Deprogramming, Brainwashing and the Medicalization of Deviant Religious Groups." *Social Problems* 29:283–97.

Schein, Edgar H.
1956   "Some Observations on Chinese Methods of Handling Prisoners of War." *Public Opinion Quarterly* 20: 321–48.

Shapiro, Robert N.
1978   "'Mind Control' or Intensity of Faith: The Constitutional Protection of Religious Beliefs." *Harvard Civil Rights-Civil Liberties Law Review* 13:751–97.

Shepherd, William C.
1978   "The New Religions and the Religion of the Republic." *Journal of the American Academy of Religion* 46, No. 4, Supplement: 509–25. Reprinted in *A Time for Consideration,* edited by M. Darrol Bryant and Herbert W. Richardson. New York: Edwin Mellen Press.

Shupe, Anson D., Jr., and Bromley, David G.
1980   *The New Vigilantes: Deprogrammers, Anti-Cultists, and the New Religions.* Beverly Hills: Sage.
1981   "Apostates and Atrocity Stories: Some Parameters in the Dynamics of Deprogramming." In *The Social Impact of New Religious Movements*, edited by Bryan Wilson. Pp. 179–215. New York: Rose of Sharon Press.

Siegel, Terri I.
1978   "Deprogramming Religious Cultists." *Loyola of Los Angeles Law Review* 11:807–28.

Spendlove, Gretta
1976   "Legal Issues in the Use of Guardianship Procedures to Remove Members of Cults." *Arizona Law Review* 18:1095–1139.

Tribe, Laurence H.
1978   *American Constitutional Law.* Mineola, New York: The Foundation Press.

Underwood, Barbara, and Underwood, Betty
1979   *Hostage to Heaven.* New York: Potter.

Vermeire, Albert R.
1981   "'Deprogramming': From the Defense Counsel's Perspective." *West Virginia Law Review* 84:91–134.

Weiss, Jonathan
1964   "Privilege, Posture and Protection: 'Religion' in the Law." *Yale Law Journal* 73:593–623.

West, Louis J., and Singer, Margaret
1980   "Cults, Quacks, and Nonprofessional Psychotherapies." In *Comprehensive Textbook of Psychiatry/III*, edited by Harold I. Kaplan, Alfred M. Freedman, and Benjamin J. Sadock. 3rd ed. Pp. 3245–58. Baltimore: Williams and Wilkins.

Wildman, Stephanie M.
1980   "42 U.S.C. § 1985(3)—A Private Action to Vindicate Fourteenth Amendment Rights: A Paradox Resolved." *San Diego Law Review* 17:317–33.

TABLE OF CASES

Abington School District v. Schempp, 374 U.S. 203 (1963).

Action v. Gannon, 450 F.2d 1227 (8th Cir. 1971).

Adamson v. California, 322 U.S. 46 (1947)

Alexander v. Unification Church of America, 634 F.2d 673 (2d Cir. 1980).

Augenti v. Cappellini, 84 F.R.D. 73 (M.D. Pa. 1979).

Baer v. Baer, 450 F. Supp. 481 (N.D. Cal. 1978).

Bavis v. McKenna, No. H-77-793 (D. Md. 1979).

Bottone v. Lindsley, 170 F.2d 705 (10th Cir. 1948), *cert. denied*, 336 U.S. 944 (1949).

Braunfeld v. Brown, 366 U.S. 599 (1961).

Briscoe v. Lahue, 103 S.Ct. 1108 (1983).

Bunn v. North Carolina, 336 U.S. 942 (1949).

Cantwell v. Connecticut, 310 U.S. 296 (1940).

Civil Rights Cases, 109 U.S. 3 (1883).

Collins v. Hardyman, 341 U.S. 651 (1951).

Committee for Public Education v. Nyquist, 413 U.S. 756 (1973).

Connick v. Myers, 103 S.Ct. 1684 (1983).

Cooper v. Molko, 512 F. Supp. 563 (N.D. Cal. 1981).

Davis v. Beason, 133 U.S. 333 (1890).

Dombrowski v. Dowling, 459 F.2d 190 (7th Cir. 1972).

Epperson v. Arkansas, 393 U.S. 97 (1968).

Everson v. Board of Education, 330 U.S. 1 (1947).

Founding Church of Scientology v. United States, 409 F.2d 1146 (D.C. Cir. 1969).

Great American Federal Savings & Loan Association v. Novotny, 442 U.S. 336 (1979).

Griffin v. Breckenridge, 403 U.S. 88 (1971).

Heffron v. International Society for Krishna Consciousness, Inc., 452 U.S. 640 (1981).

Humphrey v. Cady, 405 U.S. 504 (1972).

Illinois ex rel. McCollum v. Board of Education, 333 U.S. 203 (1948).

In re Estate of Brooks, 32 Ill.2d 361, 205 N.E.2d 435 (1965).

Jackson v. Indiana, 406 U.S. 715 (1972).

Johnson v. Stone, 268 F.2d 803 (7th Cir. 1959).

Jones v. Alfred H. Mayer Co., 392 U.S. 409 (1968).

Katz v. Superior Court, 73 Cal. App. 3d 952, 141 Cal. Rptr. 234 (1977).

Katzenbach v. Morgan, 384 U.S. 641 (1966).

Larson v. Valente, 456 U.S. 228 (1982).

Late Corporation of the Church of Jesus Christ of Latter-Day Saints v. United States, 136 U.S. 1 (1890).

Lemon v. Kurtzman, 403 U.S. 602 (1971).

Lessard v. Schmidt, 349 F. Supp. 1078 (E.D. Wis. 1972).

Marbury v. Madison, 5 U.S. (1 Cranch) 137 (1803).

Marsh v. Chambers, 103 S.Ct. 3330 (1983).

Minersville School District v. Gobitis, 310 U.S. 586 (1940).

Monell v. New York City Department of Social Services, 436 U.S. 658 (1978).

Montgomery v. Board of Retirement, 33 Cal. App. 3d 447, 109 Cal. Rptr. 181 (1973).

Mueller v. Allen, 103 S.Ct. 3062 (1983).

O'Connor v. Donaldson, 422 U.S. 563 (1975).

Olmstead v. United States, 277 U.S. 438 (1928).

Panhandle Oil Co. v. Mississippi ex rel. Knox, 277 U.S. 218 (1928).

People v. Murphy, 98 Misc. 2d 235, 413 N.Y.S.2d 540 (1977).

Perry Education Association v. Perry Local Educators' Association, 103 S.Ct. 948 (1983).

Peterson v. Sorlien, 299 N.W.2d 123 (Minn. 1980).

Prigg v. Pennsylvania, 41 U.S. 539 (1842).

Rankin v. Howard, 457 F. Supp. 70 (D. Ariz. 1978), *rev'd*, 633 F.2d 844 (9th Cir. 1980), *cert. denied*, 451 U.S. 939 (1982).

Reynolds v. United States, 98 U.S. 145 (1878).

Sherbert v. Verner, 374 U.S. 398 (1963).

South Carolina v. Katzenbach, 383 U.S. 301 (1966).

State ex rel. Swann v. Pack, 527 S.W.2d 99 (Tenn. 1975).

Taylor v. Gilmartin, 434 F. Supp. 909 (W.D. Okla. 1977), *rev'd*, 686 F.2d 1346 (10th Cir. 1982), *cert. denied*, 103 S.Ct. 788 (1983).

Tenney v. Brandhove, 341 U.S. 367 (1951).

Thomas v. Review Board, 450 U.S. 707 (1981).

United Brotherhood of Carpenters & Joiners Local 610 v. Scott, 103 S.Ct. 3352 (1983).

United States v. Ballard, 322 U.S. 78 (1944).

United States v. Cruikshank, 25 F. Cas. 707 (C.C.D. La. 1874, No. 14,897), *aff'd*, 92 U.S. 542 (1876).

United States v. Given, 25 F. Cas. 1324 (C.C.D. Del. 1873, No. 15,210).

United States v. Guest, 383 U.S. 745 (1966).

United States v. Hall, 26 F. Cas. 79 (C.C.S.D. Ala. 1871, No. 15,282).

United States v. Harris, 106 U.S. 629 (1882).

United States v. Kahane, 396 F. Supp. 687 (E.D. N.Y. 1975).

United States v. Patrick, 532 F.2d 142 (9th Cir. 1976).

United States v. Price, 383 U.S. 787 (1966).

United States v. Reese, 92 U.S. 214 (1876).

United States v. Seeger, 380 U.S. 163 (1965).

Ward v. Connor, 495 F. Supp. 434 (E.D. Va. 1980), *rev'd*, 657 F.2d 45 (4th Cir. 1981), *cert. denied*, 455 U.S. 907 (1982).

Weiss v. Patrick, 453 F. Supp. 717 (D.R.I.), *aff'd*, 588 F.2d 818 (1st Cir. 1978), *cert. denied*, 442 U.S. 929 (1979).

Welsh v. United States, 398 U.S. 333 (1970).

West Virginia State Board of Education v. Barnette, 319 U.S. 624 (1943).

Westberry v. Gilman Paper Co., 507 F.2d 206 (5th Cir. 1975).

Winters v. Miller, 446 F.2d 65 (2d Cir.), *cert. denied*, 404 U.S. 985 (1971).

Wisconsin v. Yoder, 406 U.S. 205 (1972).

Zorach v. Clauson, 343 U.S. 306 (1952).

INDEX